GYPSY JANE

**I'VE BEEN SHOT FOUR TIMES AND SERVED
THREE PRISON TERMS... THIS IS THE INCREDIBLE STORY
OF MY LIFE IN LONDON'S CRIMINAL UNDERWORLD.**

JANE LEE WITH DAVID JARVIS

JOHN BLAKE

Published by John Blake Publishing Ltd,
3 Bramber Court, 2 Bramber Road,
London W14 9PB, England

www.johnblakepublishing.co.uk

www.facebook.com/Johnblakepub **facebook**
twitter.com/johnblakepub **twitter**

First published in paperback in 2012

ISBN: 9781857826647

British Library Cataloguing-in-Publication Data:

A catalogue record for this book is available from the British Library.

Design by www.envydesign.co.uk

Printed and bound by CPI Group (UK) Ltd, Croydon, CR0 4YY

3 5 7 9 10 8 6 4 2

Papers used by John Blake Publishing are natural,
recyclable products made from wood grown in sustainable forests.
The manufacturing processes conform to the environmental
regulations of the country of origin.

All photographs from the author's collection

CONTENTS

PART TWO
PRISONS

PART THREE
IT ALL TURNED EVIL

ACKNOWLEDGEMENTS

I would like to thank the following people for help and inspiration in the writing of my book.

My son John, for all the love and care you have given me through everything.

David Jarvis, for all his hard work, help and dedication in the making of my book.

Eileen Sullivan, for all her help and support in the coming together of my book.

And everybody at John Blake Publishing for making my book possible.

Every incident in this book is totally true and I bear the scars to prove it. Names have been changed and identities obscured only in cases of legal sensitivity.

PRISON

What do you see, officer, what do you see?
What do you see when you're looking at me?
A robber, murderer, liar or scum?
Do you look at my crime and just see what I done?
Well, open your eyes, officer, you're not looking at me
Open your eyes, officer, you might get lucky and see
A girl of 16 with wings that can fly
At 18 a son who I'll protect till I die
At 20 a man who makes me happy and smile
At 30 he's gone and now I'm on trial
At 40 alone as my son has his wings
And now I'm in prison trying to kill off past sins

Jane Lee
Her Majesty's prison Bronzefield

INTRODUCTION

It was 2 November 1997 and I was lying in a hospital bed with four bullet holes in me. I should have been dead. Or at least that is what the cops told me. I was officially Britain's most dangerous woman and the King George hospital in Ilford, in the East End of London, was crawling with them. They had even drafted in the army to guard me. I don't know what they thought I was going to do in the state I was in but they weren't taking any chances, that was for sure.

I had to laugh. I was in no shape to make myself a cup of tea, let alone take on the law.

But if I could have climbed out of that hospital bed, I would have given them a run for their money. I reckon they knew that all right, which is why I was under armed guard. I was known on the streets as "the Gran", the hardest, most dangerous female criminal in the land. Shotguns, samurai swords, violence and intimidation were the tools of my trade and I was feared in the London underworld. But I was respected too because my word was my bond. And the gypsy blood in me made me wild and fearless all my life. And even if I didn't always feel that way, I had a reputation to maintain.

It had taken a Scotland Yard armed response unit to bring me down that day. Unknown to me, I had been grassed up before I attempted an £80,000 armed robbery. I was to have held up a geezer at gunpoint who I knew was a foot soldier for a Mr Big who was flogging booze illegally.

Earlier I had loaded two handguns into the back of my Sherpa van and gone out to do the job. But the law was waiting for me in numbers, armed to the teeth when they cornered me in a quiet street. I was shot through the window of my van by an officer with an M16 carbine fitted with laser sights. He got me in the hand, the arm, the shoulder, the pelvis and the back. There was blood everywhere and I told myself I was about to meet my maker – I was going out fighting... only it didn't turn out that way. Suffice to say, it wasn't one of my better days and I didn't learn my lesson even after being shot full of holes by the armed response unit.

As I lay in that hospital bed I was 32 years old and thinking about the long stretch behind bars I was facing. Until that point I had led a charmed life, having been an armed robber since the age of 14. Despite being a hard nut all my life, I was also a feminine woman and never wanted for male admirers. I was a bit of a looker in my day and turned a few heads when I wanted to. But I grew up wild in Silvertown, in the East End, and was always more of a tomboy than a girlie girl.

I am one of those people who don't know how to do handbags – and I'm not talking about carrying one. We never danced around a handbag where I come from – we only danced around sawn-offs. Shotguns, that is! If there was a problem, I tackled it head on... no chit-chat or two-faced promises. Straight down to business and to hell with the consequences, and they came quick and fast, as you will find out.

Back then I really was ready to die at the drop of a hat. That was the code I was brought up with. You had to have respect and no one did you over. And if they did, you had to make it right. I've never met a knight in shining armour but it was a matter of honour, believe me.

So how does a bird of five-foot-seven, ten-stone soaking wet, with long blonde hair put the fear of God into East End hard cases and do armed robberies? Well, when you have a gun in your hand, it carries a lot of weight. But in my case they only needed to look into my eyes to know I meant business and from an early age word got around the East End and Essex that you didn't mess with the Gran.

This is the story of how I became that woman and how I have led a life of lawlessness. I've been shot, Tasered, betrayed and served three terms in Her Majesty's prisons. And in the end I returned to my gypsy roots and went out and got my revenge on all those who betrayed me. I am lucky to have survived the bloodbaths that engulfed those who crossed me but the truth is I have been lucky all my life. It must be my Romany blood.

It isn't a pretty story but I know for a fact there isn't another woman in Britain who has had a life like mine. There is no point in pretending I'm a shrinking violet, so I'm not going to.

I've lived my life like a one-woman wrecking ball but I've taken as much as I've dished out. Even so, I'm not too proud to admit that, as a woman, a vulnerable heart has almost been my undoing. My dear old dad, Ronnie, always said to me as a kid, 'Tough times don't last, girl, but tough people do.'

I've never forgotten those words and they have served me well over the years because I am as tough as they come... and I'm still here.

PART ONE

FROM THE EAST
END TO ESSEX

1

SILVERTOWN

I have lived by the code of the old East End.
A code of honour, morals and loyalty.

Being a gypsy makes you different – and I'm different through and through. It's in my blood and that's what makes me who I am. My dad always said he was a gypsy, as were his parents, who had a horse and cart for a home. My dad's name is Ronnie. He brought me up to believe that as a gypsy you had to learn to take what life threw at you – that no matter how many times you were knocked down you had to get back up again.

'It don't matter what life dishes out, my girl. You take it on the chin and just keep going,' he would say. Simple words but wise words too. Dad is getting on now and has gone straight since the age of 30. After his final stretch he started a trade as a painter and decorator on account of him and my mum, Kathy, having me, my older sister Michelle and my brother John, who is a year older than me. I was the baby of the family.

We had a happy-go-lucky childhood and even now it takes a lot to take the smile off my face. My dad spent a lot of time inside for various bits of villainy but he did his best for us and stayed on the straight and narrow for our sakes. But he had the gypsy spirit in him. He was born on his parents' cart in 1936 and was one of ten brothers and sisters. They lived in that same cart, roaming around for the first few years of his life, until World War II came. By then they were spending a lot of time in the East End of London in an area called Custom House. Like so many other kids in the war, Dad was evacuated and ended up in Tunbridge Wells.

When the fighting was over, many gypsy families settled in the East End and that is what Dad's family did. But he never forgot he was a gypsy. It was in his blood and in his ways. He loved horses and loved to travel around. He always said that was when he felt really free. But life had changed after the war for so many gypsies. They were tied down for the first time.

Silvertown was where I grew up, in the London borough of Newham. It is a tough, industrialised district on the north bank of the Thames and is named after Samuel Winkworth Silver who opened a rubber factory there in 1852. One side of Silvertown belonged to all the factories that were built on the banks of the river and the other side is where we lived. When I was a kid, the docks were right behind our three-bed council house in

Camel Road. But all that has changed now and it's City Airport that overlooks the estate. It was nicer when I was a kid. We used to watch the ships come into the docks from our bedroom window. We would watch the dockers unloading the ships and loading them back up with different cargo before they set sail back down the river and into the sea

In those days whatever arrived on the ships in the docks for the shops of the land was always on sale in the streets of Silvertown first. There was a booming black market in the area, purely driven by the docks. There have been all sorts of regeneration projects around there but in many ways it is still the same old Silvertown to me.

I was born on 13 September 1966 and got to know the area well in the 1970s. It was so different then. There were rogues and robbers all over the place. There were all sorts of knock-off gear floating around. It was before the days of CCTV and sophisticated alarm systems and all that sort of stuff. It was much easier for anyone to go out on the rob in those days.

Silvertown was like one big happy family. Everyone knew everyone and if you didn't fit in, you didn't last long. You were soon marked out if you were dodgy. But everyone left their doors open and every house was like your own. Stealing off your own or burgling from peoples' houses had never been heard of then. How life has sadly changed for the worse.

It was in those days that I learned my values. What

was right and wrong. When you read my story, you may think I have lived by a villain's code but that is not true. I have lived by the code of the old East End. A code of honour, morals and loyalty. But as I have grown up I have realised that honour among thieves is just a fairy tale. It's sad but true that most villains don't live by the code that said we looked after our own and did what we had to do to keep body and soul together.

I remember, when I was young, going round to an older mate's house to feed her cat for her while she was on holiday. Her bloke was still there but busy doing his own things and I walked into the living room and there was this massive pallet stacked as high as me with £20 notes. My mouth just dropped open. There must have been millions there. I never touched a note though. I fed the cat and left. We were taught never to steal from our own and I never have. Although we had nothing, I had my self-respect and the trust of everyone and no amount of money would ever change that.

The next day I went back to feed the cat again and the notes were gone. I asked what happened. 'Don't worry, Jane,' he said. 'It's not even real. You should have helped yourself to a handful.' Blimey, I thought to myself. I could have got rich there and then – and I was only a nipper.

My dad had already had a family before he went to prison. He had a girlfriend named Josie who had a son they named after my dad. But Josie couldn't cope with the years of being on her own when he went to prison.

She couldn't cope with the future of visits and lonely times. I mean, two hours visiting every two weeks for years on end isn't much of a life, is it? So Dad lost his first family when he was inside. When he got out and married my mum Kathy and had us three, he vowed to go straight. He said no amount of money was worth risking his family. He said it might get hard at times – and it did – but he always reminded us we had each other.

Dad was the pushover in our house. He would always say he was going to tell Mum if we drove him mad and that would always take the wind out of our sales and quieten us. But he never did tell on us. I remember Dad once banging his head on the wall and shouting at the top of his lungs, 'You kids are driving me mad and will be the death of me.'

John and I cracked up with laughter at him until he once more said, 'Wait until your mum gets home. She'll take the smiles off your faces.'

We soon stopped laughing and started begging. As always, he never did tell. Just the thought he might grass us up to Mum got us eating out of his hand. He's a bit of a softie but us kids were blessed to have a dad so loving and understanding. That may sound odd given his criminal past but my dad is old school – a real gentleman. He knows how to treat people properly. What he wouldn't do or say to a woman, I don't expect any man to do or say to me. Dad never laid a finger on any of us. He would beat himself up instead, bless him.

I love my dad because, after Mum hit the booze, he was the saviour of our family and I was and still am his favourite, even though he denies it and says he loves us all the same. I think he loves my personality a bit more because I've got more gypsy in me than the others. Dad used to take me to the Epsom Derby in Surrey when I was little. It wasn't just for the horseracing. Gypsies from all over the land would congregate there for the races, which my dad loved, but he also wanted to remind me where I came from. 'They are your people, Jane,' he would say as I stared in wonder at all the caravans and the goings-on around the races. I used to love those trips with Dad.

Michelle, or Shell as I always call her, was Mum's favourite and couldn't do anything wrong in her eyes. She was Mum's little princess and, as John was the only son, they both loved him equally. Me, John and Shell are so close now. John was what every girl would want in a brother. He is always there for me through thick and thin. He has never disrespected me in any way and has always accepted me for who I am. Although Shell and I didn't get on as kids, we're the best of friends now. It was just sisters being silly sisters when we were young.

It was hard for my mum. She had three jobs and three kids by the age of eighteen. She worked in a factory at night and had two cleaning jobs on the go in the daytime as well. I remember Mum coming home from her night job with loads of copper strips covered in paper and we would sit for hours taking the paper off the copper before she drove it down to the local scrap yard to cash it in.

'It all helps, kids,' she would say and treat us all for helping her earn a bit extra.

She didn't just have it hard, she had it very hard and that is probably what drove her to drink. But back then us three kids just took all her hard work for granted, not realising that looking after us, holding down three jobs and keeping a home together was taking its toll. Being kids, we could only see the good stuff and not the harshness of everyday life. Mum was definitely the boss in our house. What she said was final and, if she had the hump, we all knew that we needed to keep out of her way, or else.

Mum always said I chatted away a lot like a 'little old granny'. So, crazy as it sounds, I earned my underworld nickname of the Gran very early on in life. When I started school, everybody called me Granny too – and it's true because I've always got an answer for everything. Later on in life as I developed a bit of a reputation it got shortened to the Gran.

Most people didn't even know my real name at school. It was never mentioned and I have always been Granny or the Gran ever since I can remember. If you asked anyone if they knew who Jane Lee was, people would ask, 'Who?' But you if you asked about the Gran, especially later on, and everybody knew who I was.

I was a tomboy in the clothes I wore and the way I acted. I wouldn't be playing with dolls and a pram like my sister. I'd be out making camps or playing in the factories that had closed down. And I always got on a lot better with my dad than with my mum. But there's one thing I can say about Mum. Nobody could say anything bad about us to her. It didn't matter what we'd done. She would back us a hundred per cent. Don't get me wrong. When she got us home, we would be punished but, while anybody was about, she would die before she allowed anyone to put us down.

One of the neighbours once knocked on our front door and said to Mum, 'Tell your Jane to stop playing with the ball. It has just hit my window.'

Mum was fuming. She went up to the woman's house and took her front gate off its hinges and threw it straight through her front window. '*Now* fucking moan, you silly cow,' Mum shouted as she stormed back home. That was my mum and the tough way I was brought up. As a kid, I found that episode hilarious. I couldn't stop laughing. But I got a good hiding when we got back home for laughing and for letting the ball hit the window.

Another time I'd beaten up two sisters for taking the mickey out of me. They called me scruffy and thought they were clever because they were together. I just battered the pair of them. I was always a bit handy like that for a girl. Not big and strong, just prepared to have a go. Anyway, around came their mum and dad and my mum put the fear of God into them. It got a bit physical and by the time they left they were terrified. Nobody ever complained about any of us again.

It didn't matter that money was scarce because we always ate well. Every night we had a proper cooked dinner and I've never known what it was to be hungry. There was always plenty of food on our table. Yet Mum was turning more and more to drink and that was when things started to get difficult for me. Brandy was her tipple and she couldn't get enough of it. To be honest, ever since I can remember she was drunk and, believe me, growing up in a house with a drunk who didn't mind giving me a slap made life hard. Mum was a violent drunk, I think it's fair to say. At least, that is what she became.

I was just a kid and I had a mum who was eventually drunk 24/7. She would come and beat me in the night and throw me out in the street. I'd sleep outside on the stairs in the flats opposite our house until the morning. As the years went by, I was sleeping under the flats more frequently, yet Mum was always sorry in the morning. It was tough on me. I thought Mum hated me and she was always apologetic the next day. But by dinner time she was back to being nasty and by night time she was well drunk and started getting violent again and I'd be back under the flats after getting a good hiding. Eventually, it didn't bother me. I was thinking I'd rather be there instead of being in the house with her.

There wasn't much Dad could do at the time about Mum's behaviour. Dad didn't know the half of what was going on with me and Mum. He would have killed her if he had known she was throwing me out in the night. But I couldn't tell him and cause more rows. She wouldn't do it until everyone was in bed. She would be sitting in the kitchen drinking until she wasn't herself anymore. Then some nasty violent person in a drunken rage took over. She would come for me. Sometimes I was awake and made out I was asleep, hoping she would leave me alone, but the drink just wouldn't let her.

Since Shell was her favourite and John was just John, all her bad temper and violence, was directed at me. But Mum couldn't handle me and, boy, did I bring the nutty side out in her. I didn't get on with my sister either. Shell was Miss prim and proper and didn't have a hair out of place. Unlike me, she was always immaculate and I suppose she was embarrassed about the way I was. My rough-and-tumble behaviour got too much for her and she didn't want me in her room. This was when I was eight, long before I ended up sleeping outdoors. Mum told me I had to move downstairs and sleep on the sofa. Mum said Shell needed her own room.

I didn't like sleeping downstairs as I was afraid of the dark and, being downstairs, I felt I was all on my own. I would put my head under the covers and wait for morning. I was too afraid to even peek my head back out. I was scared to death, to be honest. I started to resent Shell and Mum. So one day, when Mum was taking a nap while her hair was in rollers, I got the scissors and I cut every roller off her head. She had a big night out with Dad planned and, when she woke up, I got the beating of my life. I denied everything, obviously, but being the only other person in the house at the time – and the only one nutty enough to do it in the first place – there was no way out. But that was one beating I took on the chin. It was worth it. Mum was a bit of a dolly bird and she had to wear a wig for three months after that. And she cried like a baby. It was a sign of just how far I was prepared to go. I didn't have any limits and next on my list was Shell.

She had won a goldfish at the fair. She only had it a couple of days and I wasn't even allowed to look at it because we weren't getting on. So I waited until Mum and Shell were at the other end of the room and I grabbed it by its tail and shouted, 'Shell!' When her and Mum looked round at me, I lifted my head, opened my mouth and, while Shell screamed, 'No! No!' I swallowed it down whole in one big gulp. The goldfish went down a lot easier than the incident did with Mum. I got battered by her again but I felt it was worth it. I felt as if I'd got my own back on them both. Don't get me wrong – I'd never usually hurt an animal and never have since. In fact, I have always felt guilty about it because it was no way to treat a goldfish. I should have done something to Shell instead.

I was so strong willed that I always got on Mum's wrong side and Mum was more forceful than Dad. He tried to stop me and Mum from rowing but it was no good because he couldn't control either of us. She was a mad woman and, come to think of it, maybe my gypsy blood isn't the only thing that made me the way I am.

Mum had a babysitter called Rosie and she became my guardian angel and best friend. When she moved into the flats, I no longer had to sleep rough on the stairs. I'd just go straight to hers and she would always welcome me in her house, which became my second home.

One night, after mum turned on me, something snapped inside me and I fought back against her for the first time in my life. I grabbed her and stopped her from hitting me. I wrestled her to the ground and held her there until she calmed down. She soon stopped trying to hit me and I swore there and then that she'd never hit me again. I was so young and that was the start of living from house to house because I couldn't be under the same roof as Mum anymore. All this wasn't doing my schooling much good. I went to Cumberland school in Plaistow but, to be honest, I was never that keen and was absent more often than not. During the days I started hanging around with people who were a few years older than me because everyone my age was still at school. I practically moved in with Rosie but I also stayed with other friends that all knew Mum was boozing and losing the plot. Nobody ever turned me away. I still stayed at home sometimes but never at the weekends because that is when it could get really bad.

By this time I was growing up fast. I was already learning the street code that my dad had lived by before he went straight. I knew that you didn't do anybody any wrong unless they had done it to you first and that you didn't do any wrong to you and yours, and that you didn't make your family ashamed. I was a kid but I was already what we call old school and I was living by the rules of the East End. You don't grass anyone up and you don't do your own.

Out on the streets I grew up believing that loyalty, morals and honour were the most important things because nobody could take them away from you. You made sure you didn't give them away. And it was around this same time that what you might call my childhood came to end because I was introduced to the world of gangsters and guns – and I took to it like a duck to water.

2

SCHOOLGIRL ARMED ROBBER

I loved my sawn-off straight away.

By 1980 I was 14 and hanging around with a couple of older lads and we got into armed robberies together. How did I go from eating my sister's goldfish to pointing shotguns at people for money? Well, I'm not too sure myself. What I do know is that money was scarce, I wasn't attending school and it seemed like a good idea at the time. And you have to understand that the world I had been brought up in meant it wasn't such a big deal. Everyone was up to a bit of this and a bit of that. When you consider I was barely living at home and was fending for myself, the idea of having a few quid in my pocket was quite appealing. So where was I going to get it from? I didn't have that many options until the day one of my mates told me to pop round to his house. He was there with another mate talking about doing an armed robbery to make a lot of money. They were polishing there ~~their~~ sawn-off shotguns and asked me if I wanted in. The excitement and adrenalin had already taken over and I told them I was in all right. This was my big break. I might have only been 14 but I was a lot older than my age suggested. I had grown up fast and I was more streetwise than most other people I knew. I was trusted by everyone. It was a life-changing moment but that didn't mean it was complicated. I didn't think twice.

'I'm in, boys,' I said.

'We knew you would be, Gran. That's why we came to you.'

A few thousand pounds to a 14-year-old is a lot of money – and that was even more so 30 years ago. The prospect of a few grand made me feel like a millionaire and I loved my sawn-off straight away. It started me off on a lifelong love affair with guns. There wasn't all this CCTV stuff in those days, safes weren't on timers and we didn't come across triple-locking doors. Back then security for most businesses was a bell above the door and a mirror in the corner, and nobody ever got hurt because the staff didn't want to die heroes for nothing. We never had any bullets in the guns but they didn't know that. We weren't going out to hurt anyone. We were just doing our job and we were good at it.

I don't want to go into too many details about the jobs we did because I don't want to remind the coppers of what happened. I mean, we did a few jobs in those days and I never got caught, and I could see how the police might be a bit upset about that. So the less said about that the better. Mind you, the coppers got their payback later on so, in a way, we are all square.

On the first job I ever did, one lad stayed in the getaway car and me and the other lad put on black balaclavas in broad daylight and went inside. We pulled the guns from under our coats and, before anyone could say anything, I just pointed my gun at the man behind the counter and screamed, 'Give us the fucking money. Now!' He must have been terrified because it all went into a brown cloth bag quicker than you can say Billy Whizz and we were away on our toes, into the waiting car and gone. I was giggling when I got in the car. It was a rush and my share was around two K.

I didn't feel bad about it afterwards because nobody got hurt and it was not as if we were mugging people in the street and taking their hard-earned money. We weren't going into their homes and taking what was theirs. I mean, we did the workers at the places we robbed a favour really. They would get six weeks off work with full pay because of their ordeal if they were smart enough to play their cards right. They could have a right touch just for getting robbed by us.

By this time Mum wasn't doing any work herself. She hadn't for a good couple of years because, to be brutally honest, the drink had fucked her. What Dad was earning as a painter and decorator was getting them by but I soon found out what made Mum smile – cold, hard cash. By giving Mum money, she turned a blind eye to what she thought I was up to because she could go out and spend it on whatever she wanted to. 'Where is it coming from, Jane?' she would ask and I'd reply, 'I'm doing a bit of this and a bit of that, Mum, but don't worry, I'm doing none of the other,' and I would be gone. She didn't want to hear the truth, even though inside she guessed what I was up to.

We all kept it from Dad but don't get me wrong. He didn't go without. We just made out that Mum got the extra money from buying and selling knocked-off gear here and there. Mum was happy, Dad was happy. In fact, everyone was happy – especially me!

This went on for two years. I was no longer looking scruffy. In fact, I felt like I had it all, which meant everyone around me did, as I've always been a giver. If I've got it, you can have it as far as I'm concerned. But one day the CID turned up at Mum and Dad's door asking for me. Dad was in the pub at the time so Mum took over and said I wasn't living there, which was true enough. Anyway, Mum said she didn't know where I was and they can't have had much to go on so they went on their way.

When Dad got home and heard the news, Mum said he went white with shock. Thank God they didn't have *Crimewatch* in those days. Anyway, they had nothing on me, just some jealous local snitch giving information about what they thought was going on but didn't really know. My mates had warned me not to tell anyone what we were up to, no matter how much I trusted them. People had to be treated on a need-to-know basis and most people didn't need to know. That's how people get caught and that's why we never did. But that little visit spelled the end of my armed-robbery apprenticeship. I decided never to do another job. I knew it was coming on top and my luck would run out. I might have been wild but I wasn't stupid. Then again, life doesn't always let you do what you want.

By now Dad was getting suspicious as to what I had been up to and he searched the house for my gun but he didn't find it because it wasn't there. He said that, if the police ever found a gun in the house, they would take him away, as he was on a lifetime firearms ban for the crimes he did as a young man. That shook me up a bit. 'Don't worry, Dad,' I told him. 'My gun wasn't here. You are never going down on account of me.' I'd been keeping my gun hidden at a derelict pickle factory in Silvertown. It was well buried and I had no plans to dig it up.

3

FIRST LOVE

I was a teenage girl in love and trying to make my dreams come true.

I fell in love for the first time in my life when I was 16. His name was Jamie. He was a boxer and didn't smoke or drink. He was the opposite of me but how I loved him. He was my everything. I would dream about the day we would be married with kids – and what a dream it was.

To be honest, I thought he was too good for me and I knew he was only with me for one thing. But I didn't care. He could have it as long as he was mine. But don't get me wrong. He loved me in his own teenage, puppy-love sort of way. He was the first boy I slept with.

There wasn't a lot of money around. I was still ducking and diving but the money was nowhere near as good as I made through the robberies. I just wanted to be with Jamie all the time and, when I wasn't, he was all I could think about. It was pure, happy and in many ways one of the happiest times of my life. Jamie was a good-looking boy – really handsome – and I was an attractive young woman. Everyone said we made a lovely couple. It was a fun, fun time.

Jamie and I used to go to the pictures and we would go out clubbing sometimes but mostly we would drive down to Woolwich and watch the boats sailing from the marina. Jamie used to talk about becoming the best boxer in the country and I knew he would. I was happy. Even so, although we went out with each other for two years on and off, we were more off than on. Jamie didn't want a full-on relationship but I did. Oh, how I loved him with all my heart. We were only young and I wanted so much more so I tried to trap him. I got pregnant to keep him because I knew he wasn't ready to settle down and, to be honest, I knew he wanted a life before becoming a dad. He made it clear he wasn't ready for a family so I made out I was on the pill and got pregnant.

Looking back now, I know how selfish I was but at that time I was a teenager in love and trying to make my dreams come true. I really believed that having his baby meant he would stay with me for ever. How wrong I was. He panicked. What would he tell his family? They didn't like him being with me because of the life I had led. We came from different worlds. He said that he didn't love me but I said I was going to keep the baby anyway. He said he would stay with me until the baby was five years old. So I agreed. I thought, once we were a real family, he wouldn't leave us and he would learn to love me like I loved him. Then all of a sudden he didn't answer my phone calls. His mum came on the phone and told me to keep away from her son. I was so heartbroken and felt all alone. I never contacted him again. I just walked away. He had chosen his family over me and it was all my fault.

I told my mum and dad that I was pregnant and Dad went mad. It was bad enough being pregnant but, when Jamie wanted nothing to do with me either, that made it worse. I'd let Dad down. I understood he only wanted what was best for me and it was all going wrong. Mum was back to being nasty and I found myself pregnant and living from house to house again. There was no way I could stay at home. Mum and I had started to row and it would just be better all round if I wasn't there. I spent most of my pregnancy with a friend who shared my surname, though she wasn't related.

My friend lived in Prince Regents Lane with her family, including the mum and her husband, six sisters and a brother. They became as close to me as family and I will never forget how they looked after me when Jamie turned his back. They might not have been my blood but they were as close a family to me as my own and I thank them and love them with all my heart.

4

TOOLED UP AND PREGNANT

*I didn't want to be a gangster. I just wanted
to be a proper mum.*

After I had been pregnant for six months, I finally got
my own flat through the council in October,
1984 because of my circumstances. I'd got no money
coming in, a baby on the way and Christmas was
around the corner.

I was trying so hard to keep on the straight and
narrow but I needed money for my baby. It was time to
go and dig up my gun. I knew what I had to do and I
went and did it. I didn't want to because I had promised
myself I wouldn't do any more armed robberies after the
CID had turned up that day. But I had to do it for my
baby because I had nothing. I would just do one job so
I could make my flat a home.

The people I was robbing thought I was a gangster

but little did they know. I didn't want to be a gangster. I just wanted to be a proper mum. The job went without a hitch. But I've got to be honest, I was a lot more nervous than before because I was so worried for my baby. I used the balaclava and did the job on my own, and covered myself with a big coat so I wouldn't look pregnant. I mean, pregnancy was a bit of a giveaway as clues go, so I had to be a bit crafty on that front. But I made enough to get everything I needed for the baby's arrival. A pram, cot, baby clothes and toys, and I decorated the flat.

Dad still wasn't talking to me and, God, it was killing me because I love my dad. But I'd let him down by getting pregnant. Jamie having nothing to do with me upset Dad too because he wanted more for me. I understood Dad's feelings but I was more hurt that Dad wasn't there than I had been by Jamie leaving.

Christmas came and I had two weeks to go before giving birth. I spent Christmas with Shell, who by then was married and pregnant herself. Shell said I looked beautiful and her house was so Christmassy with all its decorations and presents under the tree. It was so lovely. Shell and I had done some growing up and she made me feel so welcome. I felt about as happy as I can remember being, apart from still missing Dad.

My son John was born on 6 January 1985 at Forest Gate hospital and, when he arrived in this world, I was the happiest woman alive. I thought a lot about Jamie and what he was missing out on but it was his loss. He only came to visit John once and I never saw him again after that.

I was going to name my son Ronnie, after my dad, but my brother came up to the hospital when all the other women were with their husbands so I said, 'John, make out you're my husband,' because I felt embarrassed about not having my own man there. So he did and, for that reason, I named my son John Ronald Lee after the two most precious men in my life.

Mum was there for the birth. I remember screaming out in pain and she grabbed my hand and said, 'Don't show me up.' I have to laugh now. She said I could go stay with her and Dad for a week so I discharged myself and went to Mum's. John was only a day old but I couldn't stay at the hospital with all the other mums. I just wanted me and my baby home and, when I got there, Dad grabbed hold of me and said he was sorry for being angry. I cried with happiness. I needed my dad – not for anything but the love he gave me.

That night Mum was completely drunk and started on me again, just like in the old days. It didn't take much to set her off and I can't even remember why she was having a go at me. But she didn't hit me any longer. She knew by now that there was another side to me and not to push it too far. But her mouth made up for it. She would say the most spiteful things and, to tell you the truth, a hiding wouldn't have hurt half as much as some of the things she came out with.

So that same night I calmly picked up John and went

home to my own flat. I loved Dad but I couldn't stay under the same roof as Mum. My baby and I didn't have much but we had each other, and I vowed there and then that my son would always have a loving home and be showered in love. I felt a love like I've never felt before. It's called unconditional love and now, for the first time in my life, I knew what it meant.

5

ALL ABOUT A BOY

*John was growing up fast. He was so handsome
and the perfect son. I was blessed when I had him.*

The next ten years were all about trying to be a mum and doing my best for John. But it didn't work out like that because, every time I tried to go straight, life took a turn. A couple of months after John arrived I met a man called Brett who was three years older than me. He was a mechanic and I fell for him hook, line and sinker. He was a handsome man with blond hair who cared for me and I was truly happy.

By this time I was 19 and the next five years with Brett were blissful, even though we had our rows. My best friend Rosie, our old babysitter, who let me stay with her when I was a kid, was there for me through thick and thin. We didn't have much but Brett, John and I were happy. We had a caravan at Canvey Island near

Southend where we had some wonderful summer holidays together. I was so happy I had found true love after Jamie. Brett was a good father to John. He really cared for him and he loved us both. But Brett wasn't very successful at holding a job down so he didn't bring much money in. We survived but life wasn't always easy.

I was hanging around with a girl named Mary and doing my best to be with John all the time. After I had been with Brett for about five years one of this girl's mates told me she didn't like what was going on at Mary's house. I asked her straight out, 'What do you mean?' She looked frightened and said she wasn't going to be the one to tell me. 'Don't play mind games with me because I don't play them. You will tell me or I'll do you.' And she did. Brett and Mary had been having an affair. I couldn't believe it. My best mate and my man.

I flew round to Mary's with a knife in my hand but she wasn't in. She was lucky she wasn't. So I went to Rosie's and by now I was sobbing. Rosie said she didn't believe Mary and Brett were having an affair and calmed me down. We had a drink, got stoned on marijuana and I said, 'She can have him.' Then Mary knocked at Rosie's door and I went for her.

I started to beat the living daylights out of her with my bare hands when she screamed, 'I wouldn't do it to you. He tried to pull me but I gave him a knock-back.' I stopped beating her when she denied it and calmed down. But later that day I confronted Brett but I didn't believe him when he denied it. He had slept with my best mate. I was certain of it. So I kicked him out of my flat. He kept begging to come back, saying he hadn't done it. He even took me to Mary's to get me to confront her again. He got her to say nothing had happened and she even said that she'd lied about him trying to pull her. I knew in my head he had cheated on me but my heart didn't want to believe it. So like an idiot I took him back. But the love had died. I tried so hard to love him after that but I hated him instead.

We moved to Rainham in Essex to try to make a fresh start and, believe it or not, I stayed with him for another five years but it didn't matter how hard he tried, what we had was dead. We got married to try to make things work but I couldn't make love to him anymore. He made me feel sick and, when he tried to touch me, I froze and I made excuses. In fact, I had a headache for five years. We used to fight all the time about it. I really tried to make myself get over it for John's sake because I wanted us to be a family but, no matter what he did, nothing could bring the love back.

He wasn't bringing in much money so I turned my hand to collecting and restoring old furniture. That was my escape. The weeks, months and years passed by and, in a way, I was happy because, by staying with him, I was keeping my family together for my son. It was only at bedtime it got bad and most of the time I pretended to fall asleep on the sofa and he would go to bed on his own. I should have left him when he betrayed me but we live and learn and, if there's one thing I learned about myself, it is that everybody only gets one chance and, if they fuck it up, they won't get another. I can take a lot on the chin – the fights and the letdowns – but to betray me... well, that's another story. I am not ever going to forgive. That's what is inside me. I'm not going to say sorry about it because it is just the way it is. I tried but it just isn't in me and I reckon there are a lot of people out there who may be able to relate to that.

I used to tell myself that Brett was what I call 'proper' but I think I always knew he wasn't that tough. Sure enough, I soon found out he wasn't. After we had been in Essex for a few years Brett and his mate rented a garage in Purfleet where they did car repairs. Brett fell out with the garage owner and was shitting himself. I knew they knew where I lived and they had my number. 'How could you be so stupid to bring trouble to our door?' I said. I asked Brett how much he owed. But now Brett was as white as a sheet and started panicking.

'You don't know them,' he said and ran out, leaving me and John.

The phone rang and I answered it. The bloke on the line asked for Brett and I told him he wasn't in. He said, 'I've told your bloke I'm coming around tonight for my money and, if he hasn't got it, I'll leave that house looking like there has been a bloody massacre.'

Well, as I listened on the phone, I wasn't happy with Brett but, at the end of the day, he was my Brett. I did exactly what my mum would have done in the same situation and protected my family. I took a deep breath and then I said, 'You come down my path and you won't ever be getting off it alive. I've got two rottweilers and a sawn-off waiting for you. Come on. Bring it on.'

He hung up on me. I hadn't got two rottweilers really. I'd got a Staffordshire Bull Terrier, Buller, and my sawn-off was buried at the pickle factory. I couldn't even go and get it as I didn't know what time they would be coming. My 15-year-old cousin Kathy was with me and she had more balls than most grown men. I knew they were coming that night at who knew what time. So Kathy and I were all alone and Brett wasn't even answering his phone. He was hiding.

Coward, I thought to myself. He had got us into a war and it was me that was going to have to stand and fight and get us out of it. I was so pissed off with Brett. By bringing his problems to my door he'd shown himself to be a bigger idiot than I thought he was.

I boiled up a big chip pan full of fat and I gave Kathy the sledgehammer while I armed myself with my samurai sword. Then we waited with my loyal Staff by our side. The Gran had taken over and I was ready for a war.

These men are scum, I told myself. Just like Brett. I mean, if you've got a problem with someone, you don't go trying to scare their bird and kid, do you? Whoever this garage owner was, if he turned up he would come proper unstuck, as I was not your normal bird. In situations like that I'm not afraid to admit I am one sicko. Especially when I think me and mine are in danger. I'm sorry but that is the way it is.

We sat up all night waiting and I love Kathy with all my heart for sticking with me. It looked like we were in an old-school war and she was as loyal as they come. After that night she became my soul mate and will be until the day we both die. I was so proud of her. But I was relieved that it hadn't come to anything. Of course, I'd have gone to war and given it my best and, believe me, a few of them would have got hurt. And yet all I wanted was to lead a violence-free life and look after my son. Oh, how I tried to have a normal, happy family. Brett phoned the next day, still shitting himself, and I told him it was safe to come home. When he got back I told him he was out of order and that he should have sorted something out before it had come to this. 'You've been asking for trouble and don't you ever bring it to my door again,' I told him. I thought how I would have died for that man when we first got together. But first he betrayed me with Mary and now he had left me to face the consequences of his falling out with the garage owner and I just didn't know how he could have done that to me. But I just told myself that he was part of my family and I would just ignore him. I was going to live with him but I didn't have to love or trust him. I knew I had to be prepared for it to happen again. I also knew that I couldn't rely on Brett for my safety, much less to bring in money. I decided that the only way was for me to start looking after myself. I'd had enough. I had tried to turn my back on crime for John's sake but life just wasn't letting me go straight. It was then that I decided to get right into guns and, believe me, I put my heart and soul into it.

I knew it was no good having a gun that was buried miles away at the pickle factory. So I went and dug up the sawn-off in case of future emergencies. I only knew a little bit about guns. Basically, I knew how to load one and pull the trigger so I decided I needed to know more. I went to my local library and got loads of books and read up. I found out that, if a gun is over a hundred years old, you can own it legally as an antique. And it can work just as well as any other gun. So you can legally own a Colt .45, for instance. Bullets, however, are not legal but I discovered bullet-making gear is legal. Shells are legal and so is the firing cap. The only thing that is not legally available is gunpowder. I needed some black powder and I got it from fireworks.

I learned how to make a bullet in ten seconds. That meant I could put together six bullets in a minute. I learned to strip a gun down to all its parts so that you wouldn't even know there was a gun in the house. In ten minutes, I could put it back together, fully loaded and working. I bought a rifle at a military fair that had been used in the Boer War. This rifle could blow a hole through a elephant but it was legal because it was an antique. Soon I had a collection of weapons – and they were all legal. I could go and put the sawn-off back in its place at the pickle factory.

Now it was time to learn how to use my weapons properly. I joined a gun club in Brentwood, Essex and quickly realised the big difference between me and most of the other members when it struck me how people went out shooting birds and animals. I could shoot wrong 'uns all day long but a defenceless animal that never hurt anyone? No, sorry. It's not me.

I wasn't that good a shot at first but with practice I got a lot better. By this time John was about eight and I soon saw that he was a natural. The boy didn't even need a sight. He just pointed and hit the target every time. I remember there was a clay pigeon show, which John entered, and he scored an incredible 39 out of 40. I was so proud. In fact, he had only missed the first one as he had never used a shotgun before and the weight of it threw him off a bit.

But more than winning competitions, the best part of our new ability was that, if we received any more threatening phone calls from dodgy garage owners – or anyone else, come to it – we were ready for a war. Now, I can hear you asking yourself – why didn't I simply call the police and let them deal with everything? Well, as I'm sure you have gathered having heard about my background, you just didn't do that. And anyway, I knew no fear. You see, blokes think us women are helpless. But, believe me, boys, there is a lot more to some of us than meets the eye. One of my friends went on a job and his gun blew up in his own hand. I've never had one blow up on me. Why? They are all tested and ready to go before I use them. Then there was the mate who did a jeweller's. This one was a success but the getaway driver had some trouble and couldn't do it so they got a replacement. But when they came running out the shop with bags of gold and diamonds and their sawn-offs, they found the car was not there. They had to run back into the shop, alarms going off everywhere, when the driver suddenly pulled up outside and they ran out, all panicking. When they asked the driver where he had been, this idiot said he had been to the shop to get a can of Coke. I think I would have shot him myself if he was on a job with me. I couldn't stop laughing. Oh, it did get funny, you know. Nothing is ever perfect, is it? We can only try our best but you do need good common sense. No education can beat a bit of common sense.

I had got myself properly armed and my cousin Kathy had moved in, as she was now my best friend as well as family. Kathy had come over to England from her home country of Ireland when she was ten or eleven. She was my saviour, as having her around made it easier to live with Brett. John was growing up fast. We hadn't got much but I hadn't done anything that could get me shot or 'lifed' off. He was so handsome and the perfect son. I was blessed when I had him. He was the most precious thing life could ever give me and I didn't want to put that in jeopardy. But Brett had been on the dole for a while after the garage incident and he couldn't provide for himself, let alone me and John. In fact, it was still the other way around. I knew I could provide if I needed to and it looked like that was the way things were going. We were paying everything between us but now I was paying it all. But for the time being I wasn't breaking the law. I was just bending the rules a bit.

Brett's sister-in-law owned a cafe and I was running it for her. Meanwhile, Kathy was looking after John indoors during the day while I was at work and we were surviving. But it's a small world and I was in the cafe one day when a rich-looking man came in. He was known in the area. He was a regular at the cafe and I'd seen him around enough to recognise him, though I didn't personally know him. But Brett seemed to – at least, he did a strange thing. He turned absolutely white, dived to the floor and, trying to stay out of sight, slipped out the back way. When I looked up again, that bloke was just standing there. He came up to me and said, 'I thought I recognised your voice. You're the bird on the phone with the sawn-off and rottweilers, ain't you?' That was when the penny dropped.

'And you're the coward that still hasn't found his balls and brought it on yet, ain't you?' I said. I had a big blade from the cafe in my hand under the counter and I was waiting for his next move. I'd come to like this man. He was respectful and it was obvious he fancied me. But although I wasn't sleeping with Brett – and I couldn't even stand him anymore – he was still my old man. To the outside world we were a normal family. I despised him but I wouldn't do him wrong. Now it seemed that the balance had changed. Bring it on, I thought. I know that was a mental thing to wish for but that was just me. Things had happened and I couldn't go back and still hold my head up, could I?

Then he said, 'Can I shake your hand, love? I truly apologise for my words on the phone. And, girl, you've got some balls on you. Most men would have shit themselves but here's a woman and she wants a war? I could hardly believe my own ears. I'm truly sorry for putting you through that. I was a bit caught out because you answered the phone instead of your Brett.'

I laughed and accepted his apology as I put the blade under the counter. But I still had to tell him straight about how I felt. I told him he was out of order by involving a bloke's bird in something she hadn't had a hand in. He accepted my reprimand like a gent and told me that Brett's garage debt had now been forgotten by way of an apology to me and that he didn't have to worry. 'He wasn't worried about you anyway,' I lied, thinking what an embarrassment Brett had become after diving for the floor and running out the back.

Then we suffered a tragedy. Rosie's ten-year-old daughter, Heather, died of a brain tumour and it crippled me. It was, and still is, the saddest thing that has ever happened to me. I went back to Silvertown and stayed with Rosie for the next two weeks. So did Paul, Rosie's brother and my lifelong friend. Me and Paul were like brother and sister but I developed other feelings for him during that time and a few months later I met him at the flat and we made love. Brett and I hadn't been together in that way for the past five years. We were together but more like enemies, just living together. Paul was one of my best friends and he made me feel special, wanted and loved. Something I hadn't felt for so long. I left Brett that same day and I've never seen him since. I also gave up working in the cafe, as it was Brett's sister-in-law's, and I was back to ducking and diving to make ends meet. I had known in my heart that this day would come from the night Brett left me and John after he received the phone call that sent him running. I had to fend for myself and I was one step away from being back in the criminal world – the same world I had so desperately tried to leave behind.

But it was Brett who had caused these problems with our once happy family, by sleeping with Mary. It was Brett who brought a night of trouble into our home. And it was the Gran who had brought the guns back into our lives for protection. Jane was slowly slipping away.

Paul, who was five years older than me, moved in but it only lasted a year. To be honest, it all got a bit ugly. We should have never got together because we ruined a lifelong friendship. To cut a long story short, I had heard that Rosie thought I wasn't good enough for her brother, which was hard to take coming from such a good friend. Rosie and I fell out over it, which I regret to this day. And if I could change anything that I'd ever done, I'd take back my row with Rosie because I lost the best friend I ever had that day. I also regret having been with Paul. Yes, we had our happy times for a while. We even got married. But he had three teenage girls by his ex and they hated me because they thought I was standing in the way of their mum and dad getting back together. The kids were wrong because Paul and his ex had been living separately for two years before I came on the scene. I would never come between a man and his woman. Paul had lived with Rosie for over a year after splitting up and by the time we got together he was living in his flat on his own. It didn't matter to the kids and that simple fact doomed my relationship with Paul.

I had told him we needed to do his flat up for the kids when they visited him there. So we did it up. It wasn't much but it was clean and homely. A proper nice flat and it was a clean place for him to see his kids. He needed somewhere like that because he couldn't see them with his ex. But the children said they wouldn't go up to the flat if I was there. One day the tyres on my car were slashed outside Paul's flat so I stopped going. Lies were being told about me to everyone, even after I'd made that shithole of a flat into a home. At the end of the day, his kids weren't babies. They were teenagers and, to tell you the truth, I'd have liked to have slapped them but I just took it all on the chin because these were Paul's kids and I knew they were hurting over their mum and dad. I understood but they did piss me off. Still, looking back, I have to take my hat off to them. The loyalty they showed their mum was priceless and I would have done the same in their position.

To make matters worse, I started getting mail from

the ex. I tried not to take any notice because she still loved him and this was her cry for help. Although I wanted to batter her, I put those thoughts out of my head because this was the mother of his kids and all that would do was make it worse for him. So I suffered it until one day I was in Prince Regent Lane in the East End, when all of a sudden the ex appeared in front of me. She had about six mates on the other side of the road. I now had a license to batter her. I never stole her bloke, I thought to myself. They split up long before I was with him. I gave her a bit of a pasting and, when I got home, the police were waiting for me. She was in hospital, they told me, and I was arrested for GBH. Would you believe it?

I told the law it was self-defence and they said Paul's ex had written a statement against me and it looked bad. I told them she was nutty and it was all lies, and I produced the letters she had sent me. They dropped the charges. But two months later I got another letter from her saying that she and Paul were carrying on behind my back. I confronted him about it and he denied sleeping with her and I believed him. He did admit going round to her house for the sake of their kids. I couldn't believe it. We had done his flat up so his kids could visit him, yet he was going to her house instead. I lost it. I started hitting him for just that reason. This woman had sat in a police station and written a statement against me and he was still in contact with her. He'd betrayed me and by now I knew I could never forgive a traitor. What a disappointment he had turned out to be. It was over. I'd looked up to this man, trusted him and would have died for him, and he wasn't what I believed he was.

I knew he was hurting about our break-up but he was out of my life for good. I was gutted and sad but I knew there was no going back. But then one day I was told he had accused me of grassing him up after the police pulled him up on his bike for stealing scrap metal. I couldn't be sure he had said it, but I had a reputation to protect. To make things even worse, by then I had got my fingers in a lot of criminal pies. I went mad. Call me what you like but not a grass. Nobody believed him but it had been said and I had to defend my reputation. If he had said it, he couldn't have realised how far I would go to protect my name. He thought that, because I loved him, I wouldn't blow him away. Well, sorry, I love my reputation more. I went home and got my guns. I was going to war. I was going to blow his fucking head off. I'd had enough.

I knew he was living at the flat we had done up and I set myself up in the flats opposite with a sniper's rifle. It was an M16 carbine with three settings. Automatic, semi-automatic and single shot. I had it on the single-shot setting because I had a bullet with Paul's name on it. I know it was mad. But I wanted to kill him. He wasn't there and I waited for days but then I was spotted. It soon got around that it was me in the flats opposite with the rifle and now Paul was saying I was a hit woman but I didn't care. As I said, call me what you like apart from a grass. And anyway, 'hit woman' had a sort of ring to it. Luckily for him, I never saw him. And I've never seen him since. The marriage was over. That's one relationship I regret, as we were the best of friends all our lives and a lifelong friendship was ruined within a year. But time is supposed to heal everything and I even came to regret the way we split. I have no hard feelings towards him now. I wish him and his family all the happiness in the world. Maybe this had only been retribution anyway. I believe God pays debts without money. I was still with Brett when I slept with Paul so this was payback.

I was still OK. I had my son and we were very close. John was growing into a handsome young man. He was a lot like me in many ways. He was so loyal and his personality was amazing considering he was an only child. He didn't have a nasty bone in his body, even though I spoiled him rotten. He had a heart of gold. Don't get me wrong. If you mess with him, he will do you. That's how he was, just like me. But if you were good to him, he would die for you. Everybody loved him though.

I had only given birth to one child, yet it was like I had a hundred, as John's mates practically lived at our place. I bought him a caravan and parked it on the drive. It was like the local youth club in there. They had a stereo, PlayStation and everything they needed, and they loved it. It was better than them walking the streets, in my book. He was happy and that was all that mattered.

I was on my own though, money was short and, to tell you the truth, I was bitter. As I've said, I always knew there was another side to me but now it was out and here to stay, at least for a while. If there's one thing I always tell people it's that there were two of me. There was Jane and there was the Gran. And my advice to them was to be friends with Jane and not enemies with the Gran. Jane will love you, look after you, help you and never do you wrong. The Gran will shoot you or stab you. She will destroy you and love every minute of it. The choice was yours. It wasn't that I wanted to be the Gran. Life just didn't seem to let me be Jane.

I was told about a particular security guard who regularly took some £10,000 from businesses to the bank. I watched him for a couple of weeks before I took on the job. It was a success but I will be honest – I just about got away with that one by the skin of my teeth. After I grabbed the money bag, the guard started chasing me and he was not only bloody fast but seemed to have forgotten about my sawn-off. Now there was one man who did actually have balls. But I just made it to the car ahead of him and sped off. I couldn't believe he had come after me. I mean, I hadn't wanted to shoot him. Not really. On my jobs a shooter was just there as a deterrent. You never really wanted to use it. Anyway, I got away with it. Just.

I had just bought a car for £2,000 and I was able to pay off that debt. I paid the bloke who gave me the information and I ended up with £5,000 left over. With that I bought a kilo of speed and a kilo of puff to sell on. I always liked puff myself, as it calmed me down – not a bad property for it to have in my case. When my world seemed like it was surrounded by barbed wire and thorns, I had a smoke and everything turned to roses and lilies. It was an illusion, I know, but sometimes, when everything is dark, who can blame you for putting the lights on, even if it's a false light? It helped and, God, by now I needed a bit of help. Some people's vice is drinking but mine was always puffing.

Now the Gran was really taking over because Jane couldn't cope anymore. Everything she did just got stamped on and abused so I had to put her away where nobody could hurt her. If anybody tried to hurt the Gran, well, it would be their funeral.

6

THE BEER RAN OUT

It was a big, fuck-off weapon. It had a curved blade and a big handle because it was designed to be used two-handed, just as the Japanese samurai warriors used it.

'That's a lot of booze you've got in the back of your van,' the customs official said as I sat behind the steering wheel of my yellow Transit van and waited to drive onto the Eurostar in Calais.

'I'm getting married,' I said. 'We're stocking up for the reception. It's all for personal use and it's much cheaper buying it this way.'

'Funny that,' he quipped back. 'I reckon that must be the tenth time you've got married this month from what my colleagues tell me. You're going backwards and forwards like a jack in the box.'

'I keep falling for the wrong man and my plans keep changing,' I said with a grin. I was behind the wheel and a good mate was sitting next to me in the passenger seat.

She was also trying hard not to laugh. We were on the beer run. It was just like doing the booze cruise, only we were doing two runs a day, buying in bulk and selling the booze and fags to dodgy warehouses and off-licences who didn't want to pay import duty. It was the best money I had ever made and I didn't need my sawn-off. I felt sorry for Tracey because her husband had been cheating on her and one month before Christmas in 1995 he just did one and disappeared, leaving her and her four kids with nothing.

I had got into the beer game after one of my mates asked me to work for him. He was doing it, needed a driver and said he would pay me £50 a journey. I could do two trips a day for seven days a week if I wanted. It was good regular money so long as I didn't get caught. I was already earning a few quid through the speed and the puff but I could always do with some more money. I was on my own now and you never knew when times would become hard again. While it's there, grab it. I snatched his hand off.

John was ten by now and I had turned twenty-eight. Life had been hard but nothing I couldn't deal with. At first Tracey took over at home looking after my boy while I'd do two journeys a day, seven days a week. It just went to show I didn't mind doing some graft because it was hard. But I was supporting my boy and looking out for our future and I was happy with the work. In fact, I enjoyed it. The bloke I was working for was one of my mate's husbands and I thanked her for trusting me with him on the road. She wouldn't have let just anyone go with her fella but she knew I was proper. She said, 'Jane, if there's one person I know I can trust, it's you.' She asked me to keep my eye on him though and we both laughed.

The business relationship was good for the first few months, apart from the frequent occasions when I had to lend him the money to get the beer due to unforeseen circumstances. Basically, he was skint most of the time. I didn't mind at first. But then I found out he was on crack cocaine and the money was going on his filthy habit. So I told him, 'I'm not laying out all my money every day and doing all the work for £50 anymore. I want in on the profits and, if my money is making the profits, half of it is mine.' He didn't like it but he had no choice because, if I pulled my money out, he wouldn't even have a business.

Then I found out he'd got a bird on the side. Now, I loved his missus – she was a true friend of mine who had put her trust in me. She had six kids and was living off benefits because he didn't give her anything. In fact, he was even taking money off her to spend on crack with his other bird. I grew to hate him. I couldn't tell his missus though. I couldn't be the one to make her life more sad than it was already. But he knew I didn't like what was going on. The crack had him in its grip so bad that he even lost his van over it.

I bought my own transport and before too long he was working for me. I was on a roll and life was finally being good to me. All I needed was to avoid being nicked. Tracey was still playing Mum and she did everything from looking after John to sorting out the bills, cooking and cleaning – everything really. I paid her well and she had whatever she wanted. The cash was rolling in. I was tired all the time but I was living and I was not being let down by some bloke being all mouth and no trousers.

I was not only the only women doing the beer run, I was the first. That may never go in the *Guinness Book of Records* but it remains a fact I am proud of. There would be 50 vans all driven by men. Don't get me wrong. I wasn't a lesbian but at this moment in time I was no lady. I was all woman though and some of the men tried to pull me. But I'd had enough of blokes by this time. It was me keeping house and home together and I didn't want anything to rock the boat now that everything was looking like plain sailing. The blokes soon found out it was a mistake to get too friendly. I was there to do a job and get home to my John. End of.

'Hello, darling. What's a good-looking girl like you doing a job like this for?' was a typical chat-up line. I would get it all the time. But I was very bitter, to say the least, and I blamed all men for the way I had been treated. I knew it was wrong but the Gran was out and in charge, and any man paying me a compliment or trying to get too friendly with Jane was likely to get the Gran answering him back.

'Who the fuck are you talking to? What's a fucking

div like you doing a man's job for?' I didn't make myself very popular but it worked. They couldn't say a nice thing to me. They thought I was mad. In a way, I suppose I was, or at least single-minded. They usually knew from looking in my eyes that I wasn't interested. A lot of people have said there was something in my eyes that showed I meant business.

'Don't look at me like that, darling,' they would say.

'Like what?' I would reply. I knew very well what that look was. It was hard. I didn't always know I was giving it. But there could be a message in my eyes. It was my gypsy blood and the life I had led. I was five-foot-seven with long blonde hair and a figure to die for. I really looked good but I was a hard bird by now and it was going to take a lot to make me melt. And, just in case any of those drivers weren't getting the message and fancied their chances with me, I kept my samurai sword in my cab. I never had to use it though. Well, not on a driver because they just knew that one word back from them after I had warned them would result in severe repercussions.

My crack-addict mate continued to let me down by not turning up for work. But his little trips to see his other bird didn't cause a problem once I had my operation up and running. In many ways I was glad to see the back of this bloke, as I'd had enough of his sort and how they treated women. He'd got me into the beer run – I was grateful for that – but that was about as far as it went.

I got one of my good friend's two teenage girls to look after John indoors. They were 16 and 17 and their mum and dad were always on call if they were needed. John was loving it. He could have his mates stay and I supplied anything they needed, plus I was paying the girls a couple of hundred quid a week and they were more than happy. Things were running smooth and everyone was happy. For the first time in ages I could spend money. I was collecting antiques and I really got into it – furniture mostly. And I'd bought every bottle of champagne you could get, plus perfumes. I still had my collection of guns – all legal – knives and swords, and jewellery. And I'd bought everything myself – all the things I had always wanted but until now I could never afford. Nobody, apart from Rosie, had ever bought me anything when I was a little girl. Now my house looked like it was an antique shop with antiques piled everywhere.

On one day off I went shopping in London at a military shop but arrived after closing time. I just knocked on the door and, when the man came to say he was closed, I pulled out a big wad of £50 notes and waved it at him. You should have seen his face. He couldn't unlock the door quick enough. There was me in my army trousers and bomber jacket and Doctor Martens boots. I felt good with a pocket full of money. Next I went into Jane Norman in Oxford Street and, even though I don't wear dresses, I thought they did look pretty. I bought eight dresses and two jackets and it came to over £2,000. I just put the cash on the counter in front of the startled assistants. I had a good figure in those days and those dresses looked good on me. Even after all my relationship problems, I wondered if a special man would come along and see me in them. But for the time being it was just nice to have enough money to be able to afford them.

I wasn't the only one who was happy. John was loving it because he could have anything he wanted and, as long as he was happy, I was happy. I bought him a couple of 50cc schoolboy motorbikes and all the top games. I was spoiling the both of us. I know it sounds like I wasn't spending a lot of time with John but I was doing what I could. I was a women living in a man's world and I tried to spend as much time as possible with him when I finished work. But I was worn out. Usually, I would get home in the morning after a run and take John and all his mates to Southend, where I would buy them all lunch, give them money for fair rides and then I would crash out on the beach. Afterwards, John would come and wake me, we would all have dinner and then go home. It was crazy. I mean, I wasn't sleeping in a bed, I was sleeping on Southend beach but, if meant I would have more time with my John, it was worth it. And we were all happy.

It wasn't the perfect way to bring up your child but I was doing my best. He never moaned. He was the most handsome and perfect son. John and his mates even came to France with me sometimes. I paid them £30 each and they loved it because it was a bit of extra pocket money and a bit of an adventure. They worked really hard, loading and unloading. But I never let them come when they should be at school – only at weekends and on holidays. John didn't even have to earn the money, as I gave him whatever he wanted but, being like me, he was keen to get stuck in and he worked as hard as any man I know. I was so proud of him – and still am.

The man I had started off with on the beer run soon wanted to come back to work with me when word got around about how well I was doing. But I wasn't having it. I knew he was still treating my friend – his missus – and her kids like dogs. He was never at home and never paid the bills. I didn't like it and I knew he thought that, because he was six feet tall and twenty stone (of fat), he could intimidate me. He tried anyway.

He came round and, before he was through the door, he started shouting about how I owed him. He thought that, because he could intimidate and scare his missus, he could do the same to me. I just picked up a bottle of spirits and smashed it across his head. He dropped to his knees and there was claret everywhere. Being hit with a full bottle is the same as being hit with a hammer but he was still screaming abuse so I grabbed another and did him again. Down he went for a second time but he got up, still shouting, 'You mad bitch!' and he came at me. But by now I'd grabbed my samurai sword and he turned in panic and ran for the door. At that point Tracey turned up. She took in this 20-stone idiot, blood everywhere, and me chasing him with my sword. The red mist had definitely descended. I know I might sound nutty but the people I was involved with were total villains – and he was the worst. He was off his head on crack and had no morals or honour and no loyalty to anyone. Everything I hated in a man. I wasn't around innocent people with normal lives.

He got to his car just in time. As he slammed the door I smashed the blade straight through it. 'Don't you ever come back and threaten me in my home, you fat bastard!' I shouted as he sped off down the road.

Tracey told me to get some sleep and she cleared up the mess. The next day I was on my way back to France when a mate phoned to say word had got around the East End about me smashing this bloke up with the bottles and my sword. Apparently, the coward was going around saying it was lucky I was a woman or he would have of done me good and proper. That was a mistake on his behalf. I couldn't ignore the insult. This was just the world I was in and it was how I survived. It was mad and sad but it was life in that world. I was in danger of losing respect and then I would stop earning, and I couldn't allow that to happen.

I had John and his mate with me in the car but I turned round and started heading for his crackhead's house. He wasn't there so I went to his mum's house and he wasn't there either but it wasn't too long before he turned into the street in his car. I pulled out my sword and John's mate looked a bit shocked. I mean, this sword was the business. It was a big, fuck-off weapon. It had a curved blade and a big handle because it was designed to be used two-handed by Japanese samurai warriors.

'What are you going to do?' John asked.

'Watch and learn,' I said.

I jumped out of my van, ran to his car door and held the blade to his throat. 'Don't you ever come to my house again or tell people what you are going to do to me, you fat bastard!' I screamed at him. 'If you do, I will cut your fucking head off.'

He screamed like a girl, this 20-stone hard man. 'Please don't. We've been mates for years, Jane,' he whimpered.

'I'm lucky I'm a woman or you'd have done me? You pathetic piece of shit,' I smirked at him. 'You had better start looking at me as a warrior because I'm the most dangerous woman or man you're ever going to meet.' I left him there sobbing and begging for his life and got back in my van and carried on to France to do my day's work with the lads.

John and his mate just looked at me, then looked at each other and burst into laughter. 'It's better than going to movies, watching you perform, Jane,' John's mate said. We did laugh about it. Another funny thing was that the crackhead's brother was a good mate of mine. You may think he would be on his brother's side in all this but he thought I had done the right thing by teaching him a lesson. I used to visit him at his home in Kent on the way back from France. I'd pop in just to have a bit of a break from the driving. 'You done the right thing with my brother Jane,' he said one day. 'He needed teaching a lesson and you done that good and proper.'

After a while the beer run started to take its toll on me physically and I was starting to fall asleep at the wheel. But I wanted to keep getting the money in while the going was good. There was no way I wanted to slow down now I was on top. Like a mug, I started taking speed to keep me awake, going for days without sleep. I'm not making excuses. All I can say is that it worked. It made more sense than one of the staff at a warehouse in France I used, who tried to have me over on the money. I mean, they tried to steal from me and for a little while they got away with it. You see, they had these counting machines that checked you had paid them the right amount. There was no need, from my point of view. I would always check the amount before I left home in the morning. When I got there, I would just give it to them and they would stick it in their machine and it was always right. But one day there was a new bloke taking the money. I had given him £1,500 and he put it in the machine, then said I was £40 short. This was a first but I was tired because I'd been doing two trips a day for months now and I was lucky to get fifteen hours sleep a week. So I put this down to tiredness, apologised and gave him the difference.

But on the next trip the same thing happened. 'You are £60 short this time,' he said. I gave him the extra but I wasn't amused. I knew I hadn't made two mistakes on the trot and I was certain he was having me over. If there were two things I never got wrong, it was what I had to pay out and what I got in. But I just suffered again, although I know I should have counted the money by hand in front of him. So I took that one on the chin but I made up my mind he wouldn't do me again.

Two of my mates counted the money with me before I left for the next trip. One at a time we each did it. And it was there, every penny. When I got to France, I gave this bloke the money and he put it in the machine and, lo and behold, it was £40 short. I already knew what I was going to do. My sword was sheathed inside my bomber jacket in the middle of my back. I reached round for the handle over my shoulder and pulled it out. You should have seen his face. I didn't say anything. I just chopped him across his shoulder and he fell to the floor, screaming like a pig. I didn't want to kill him but I did want to hurt him and show him what happens to lying thieves. He'd thought that because I was a woman he could have me over. The idiot. Out of everyone using the place, all the men, I was the worst and most dangerous person to have over.

And he had just found that out the hard way. There were about eight men behind me waiting to be served but they just bowed their heads. Not one of them said a word to me.

My beer had been loaded so I grabbed the money, jumped in my van, where Tracey was already sitting, hid my sword and put my foot down because now I needed to get out of France. I had known what I was going to do to him but it wasn't until I'd done it that I realised what an idiot I'd been. I mean, I was in France and I had just stabbed a Frenchman, and now I had to get back to England sharpish. Yet I didn't regret what I'd done for a moment. I was old school and I didn't call the police – not that I was in a position to. I dealt with it myself. That was my way. You fucked with me, I would be your judge, jury and executioner. As it was, I made it home without any problem from the police. I reckoned the guy I stabbed was about as interested in calling them as I was. And I like to think I was the last person he played that dirty trick on.

There were about 50 vans in line for the journey back over the Channel but, while mine was old, it was special. The last owner had been a police officer so, accidentally on purpose, I left his name on the paperwork. I thought it might make me untouchable. What copper is going to pull another copper? As we waited to get home, the van in front of me started rolling backwards and hit us. I was with a good mate and said, 'Look at this idiot. He's going to hit us.' It seemed very funny – I mean, hysterical – by the time it hit us because I was high on puff. The man got out of his van. I was nearly crying with laughter when I said, 'You hit us but don't worry, there's no damage.' I couldn't even get out of the van I was laughing so much. But he was looking a bit puzzled.

Then he said, 'No, love. Vans don't roll up hill. You've hit me.' That finished us off. We just couldn't stop laughing. It was the puff. We were out of it and it was only luck that we didn't get pulled over. The bloke just walked away shaking his head and, fortunately, laughing to himself. There was no harm done. We laughed for weeks afterwards over that.

Another time, we were on the train, fully loaded, during the day and we went to the toilet. When we got back to the van, there were about 20 men up against the van pushing it. I'd forgotten to put the handbrake on and it had rolled into a convertible BMW, denting the back end. I apologised to the owner of the car but he said, 'That's OK, sweetheart. My motor's only an old peace of shit. No real harm done.' Flash git, I thought to myself. A motor worth £25,000 and he's calling it a 'piece of shit'.

When we once had 500 cases of lager in the van, a friend and I were driving home and all of a sudden there was a massive crashing noise. I had fallen asleep. We had veered out of our lane and hit road cones in the middle of a section of road works – and thank God we did because, if we had stayed in our lane, we would have driven into the stationary traffic ahead and probably been killed. Instead, we were in the works lane smashing cones all over the motorway. We were suddenly wide awake and I couldn't get out of the works lane because there were cones stuck under the van and everyone was looking. I just looked at my friend and drove right through them. It did us a favour really because we missed all the traffic and got off the motorway. But it was scary too. When we got home, we still had a cone under the van but I was so exhausted that I just went to bed.

I could only think that the Billy wasn't working as well it had, as there is only so much your body can take before it needs rest. I was working constantly and battling through the exhaustion. It wasn't just the money. By now people were relying on me to get their orders in. We were lucky we hadn't died that night but the Billy took those thoughts away and it was all about getting the job done.

On the next trip the van decided to break down on the way home. It was fully loaded, we were on the M20 on a steep hill and the van was doing about five miles an hour before it died on us. We were nearly at the top of the hill on the hard shoulder when it overheated for the last time. The journey was just getting too much for the old vehicle. So we let it cool down a bit. We kept trying to start it again but it wasn't having it. I stuck it in reverse, took my foot off the brake and let it roll backwards down the hill. We were going backwards on the hard shoulder of the M20 at about 50 miles an hour, fully loaded. It was flying – but in the wrong direction. There were lorries flying past us with drivers just gawping in amazement at how fast a Transit van could go in reverse down a hill. But we were terrified and those drivers must have been too, seeing us heading in their direction at breakneck speed. I mean, we could have veered across into their path at any second. We were in big trouble. If I couldn't keep it in a straight line, we were dead. But, amazingly, I got it to bottom of the hill and we rolled to a stop. I tried to start it again but the engine was still dead. We could see a petrol station in the far distance across fields and hills.

I said we had to get to the garage to get some water for the radiator but my mate replied, 'Leave it out, Jane. I'm knackered and it looks miles away.'

I told her to stop being a baby. 'You're a soldier tonight, girl. We've got a dodgy load of booze so we've got to get this van started and get home or we could end up being nicked.' We climbed the barrier into the fields, walked through a forest, got to the garage and she had been right. It was a lot further than it looked. Even then we had to wait two hours for it to open. We bought loads of bottles of water and went back to the van and poured the water into the radiator. And, thank God, it started and we headed home.

What a life we were having. It was hard work and

scary when we broke down in the middle of the night. But we were earning and we were surviving. That's life, I thought to myself as we got back to Essex.

7

THE LOVE OF
MY LIFE

*So that is how I met my Matt – doing a drug deal for
quarter of a kilo of Billy in the Kent countryside.*

I hardly know where to begin telling you about Matt.
It sounds like a cliche and it is a cliche but he was
the love of my life. As usual with me and men, things
took a turn for the worse but it is true to say that Matt
is still in my heart and will be until the day I die. I can't
see any other man changing that now. I wasn't to know
when I met him on a fine summer's day in the Kent
countryside in 1995 that he would become such a
massive part of my life, and that the end of our love
affair would lead me to plot four murders. And I
couldn't know then that he himself would meet a
violent end and throw my world into turmoil. But by
now violence was becoming an occupational hazard
with me. The world I was in was the only one that

offered me a way to support John and, as far as I was concerned, that was the end of it.

One day, on the way back from France, I popped in to my mate's house in Kent for a cup of tea and a chat, just to break the journey up and – wow! – there was Matt standing in the front room. He was big, strong looking and handsome, and he had an air about him. Confidence, I suppose you would call it. He was sure of himself, all right. You know, looking back now, I think it was love at first sight but, given everything I had been through with men, I wasn't about to admit that to myself straight away. I mean, I'd only popped in for a cup of tea and my knees had gone weak and my heart was going pitter-pat. I had to fight it. I pretended not to like Matt in the beginning. As it was, I mistook that self-confidence for arrogance at first. And I'd been let down by men who thought that, just because I was a bird, they had something over on me. By now I knew different and was behaving accordingly at every opportunity. No bloke was going to dominate me just because he was male. He had to have something to back it up. I was no pushover. I wanted the love and care that so many other women had and, above all, I needed real loyalty because it was betrayal that had ruined all my past relationships.

Matt was a giant, yet as calm as you like. He was waiting for some Billy, which hadn't arrived and, when I got there, he was having a bit of a moan. He was saying to my pal, 'You're bloody useless, mate. Where's my gear? I got people to see and places to go. I can't be sitting around here all day chewing the fat with you. Know what I mean, son?'

It was as if I wasn't even in the room. I thought to myself, he fancies himself a bit. I wouldn't let him talk to me like that. But at the same time, I couldn't take my eyes off him. I was just about to pipe up in my mate's defence and it was as if my mate could read my mind – he gave me a look. It was a kind of gesture which said, 'Leave it, Jane. Don't mess with this geezer.' Well, I was dealing in a bit of Billy in those days and, since I could see the problem, I thought I could help him out and I knew my mate knew that. So I bit my tongue until he gave me the nod.

'Jane here might be able to help you out, Matt,' my mate said. Can you do my very good friend Matt here a quarter-kilo of speed, Jane?'

Well, that cheered me up straight away and I agreed, especially as I'd only popped in for a cup of tea. That was a £1,250 deal and a nice little earner. I told him I was putting £500 on top as my earner but Matt insisted on giving me £750 – well over the odds – for helping him out of a spot. I liked his style. Even so, I told Matt I thought he was a bit full of himself. 'But now that I've earned this money off you, I must say, you're not that bad, are you?' I joked.

'If I'm not that bad, can I take you out then?' he came back as quick as you like and I agreed immediately. I couldn't see the point in pretending. I had never met a man I had felt so instantly attracted to. He was direct and I liked that in a man. He took after my own heart. We exchanged phone numbers and Matt said he would call me in a couple of days. I was excited by him. I could tell he was dangerous and cocksure. And, of course, he was a villain. But I had done the loyal mother-and-provider bit for so long that I reckoned I was entitled to bit of excitement. I was tingling all over when he left but I tried not to show it.

'Listen, Jane, I know you like him,' my mate said. 'The electricity in the room as soon as you walked in said it all. But Matt is a bloody nutter so you are going to have to be careful of him. I don't want to see you get hurt.'

I said to my mate, 'He's a nutter? What about me? I'm a bloody nutter too and he might need to be careful of me. Anyway, he is just the way I like them... big and good looking and with a bit about him.' And, oh my, did Matt have a bit about him. He was six-foot-six and twenty-five stone of solid muscle. Now I know that may be hard to believe but that was him. He trained at his own gym all the time and he had muscles everywhere. They used to say he had muscles on his ears. Think of Arnold Schwarzenegger and you begin to get the idea. He had a home in Kent, near Ashford, but I think he spent more time in the gym than he did at home, to be honest. All he told me was that he came from Omagh, in County Tyrone, Northern Ireland but had settled in Kent. He bought and sold expensive sports cars, dealt in drugs, had a little security operation for clubs and gigs and kept Alsatians and a rottweiler. He had his fingers in a few pies and was doing very well for himself.

So that is how I met my Matt – doing a drug deal for a quarter-kilo of Billy in the Kent countryside. Or should I say, Mad Matt? That was his nickname because there was nothing he wouldn't do. He was fearless and a bit crazy with it. Two days later he rang me and we made a date. It was my 29th birthday in a couple of days so we decided to go out and celebrate.

On my birthday he pulled up outside my place in a Porsche. A Porsche! And because I told him on the phone I was into antiques, he had bought me a few things for my birthday. In fact, his car was full of presents – among them a beautiful bunch of red roses. My favourite flower. I couldn't believe it. He made me feel so special. I felt on top of the world and I thought my dad was going to be so proud of me. I knew Matt was a villain but that was my life and Dad knew it too. Matt took me to a beautiful restaurant in Kent. I hadn't felt like this about anybody for a long time. After the meal we went back to my place and I couldn't believe the words I was hearing. 'I've had a wonderful time, Jane,' he said to me. 'You're not like all the rest. You are so beautiful and you've got some personality on you. I never know what you are going do or say next and I like that. I like it a lot.' He took me up to my bedroom and we made love. After the years of struggle and disappointment, I let everything go. For that night I was a woman who didn't have to be strong anymore. I knew

I was falling in love big time and, boy, did I feel happy about it.

Those first few weeks went particularly well. He treated me like a lady whenever we met and, not only did I adore him, but I looked up to him because of the way he conducted himself. He never went looking for any trouble but you had that feeling he could handle it if it came looking for him. He lived in Kent and I was still busy doing the beer run so it is wasn't even as if we had to be in each other's pockets, which I think was a good thing in those early days. I also thought that one of the first rules of falling in love was never to mix business with pleasure but, with me and Matt, things were a little bit different because it was business that brought us together – the drugs business, that is. But then it did cause a problem.

He asked me for some more Billy but I didn't have enough. He wanted a kilo and my usual contacts didn't have that amount of gear. Matt played in the big league compared to me, I've got to be honest here. And that was one of the things that impressed me about him. I fancied him, all right. He brought excitement. I didn't want to let him down so I had to go through another contact, which I didn't like doing, normally. But I set it up and the new guy gave me a sample of the gear and it was good. So I did the deal and got the gear for Matt and, after paying me for it, he took it back to Kent.

Everything seemed fine until Matt phoned me later that day. 'This gear is shit, Jane,' he said. 'You've been had over, which means I've been had over and I am not happy. I'm out five K. They gave me a good sample but then they switched the main delivery for a load of shit.'

I wasn't happy at the news either. 'Bring it back here, Matt,' I said, 'and I'll give you your money back straight away.'

Matt came over and handed me the dodgy gear and I gave him his money back. 'What are you going to do?' he asked.

'I'll sort it,' I said. 'Don't worry.'

'No, I'll sort it. I don't want you getting in too deep on my account. This could be trouble,' he said, putting his hand on my shoulder, all protective.

I knew he meant well but my independence had become so important to me. I had learned to rely on myself through thick and thin and, as much as I was already coming to love and trust Matt I knew he wanted to look out for me, I found it hard to stop looking out for myself because that was how I had survived so far. I looked up at him with loving eyes and said, 'Now, look here, lover boy, I'm a big girl and can handle it. How do you think I managed before you arrived on the scene? Leave it to me, Matt.'

But he wasn't happy. In fact, that was the understatement of the century. Matt was old school and he didn't want his bird doing what he thought was his job. It would be fair to say he had the right hump with me for turning down his offer of help and him having the hump was giving me the right hump too. We started to argue.

'Tell me who they are!' he shouted. 'You aren't going nowhere. I am not having my bird running around getting nicked.'

I wasn't having it. 'Now, listen to me, Matt. I don't need your help or anybody else's. Do you understand me? You can't tell me what to do.' He was fuming but he didn't say another word and just stormed out of my house. I was upset but the last thing I wanted was more arguments. I had got myself into this mess and I would get myself out of it. The day I started letting other people fight my battles for me would be the day I stopped being me and I couldn't have that. It would be bad all round. Matt still had a lot to learn about me.

I got my guns and I went to see the middleman who had done us over. Once in his house, I told him the gear wasn't the same as the tester he gave me. I didn't want to start off heavy. 'I want my money back, mate, simple as that,' I said. 'I'm not happy. I've just rowed with my Matt over this.' He looked scared but it wasn't me he was worried about. He told me he hadn't got my money and that he had bought the gear off someone else. He had been done over too.

'Take me to them,' I told him.

'These are proper gangsters, Jane. I'm not too sure about fronting them about this. They'll kill you. It's some crew from Essex. There is nothing you or me can do.'

But I don't scare that easily. 'I don't care if it's the fucking Kray twins themselves who are behind what has happened. No one's having me over. Fucking take me to them.'

He couldn't decide whether he was more scared of them or of my guns. In the end, he took me, bringing his brother along as muscle. We ended up at a pub and, while my middle-man went inside for a quick sneak preview, we waited for him to come back out. He told us there were about 30 of them in there. 'Leave it, Jane. It's fucking suicide. They're drinking and tooled up. I know this crew. Leave it, babe.'

I didn't hesitate. 'Let's get in there then,' I said. I started walking and he followed me. Once again, I wasn't sure if he was more frightened of me or them.

The gangsters were all in their suits, looking well flash. Me? I was in my army gear – combat trousers, DM boots, green T-shirt and bomber jacket. My 9mm Browning automatic pistol was in one pocket and my German Mauser pistol was in the other. My pal pointed out the boss and over I went.

I told him straight that I wanted my money back. 'You sold shit gear to him,' I said, nodding at my pal. 'And he sold it to me and I sold it to someone very important to me. So give me my money back and we can call it quits.'

His boys all stopped what they were doing. I'd got their attention now. You might think I was frightened at this point or in over my head. But I felt totally in control, razor sharp and ready for them. I knew they wanted to have a go. Me being a bird, they would think I was easy but I was double ready. The boss's boys were looking a bit puzzled, as if to say, 'Look at the brass neck on it.' All the same, they started making to get their tools out. When the boss himself said, 'Get this lady away from me,' I knew it wasn't going to be civilised. Yet I already knew I had one thing in my favour – his words meant he had underestimated me and I knew that also meant he was slow off the mark.

Before he had even finished speaking I'd pulled my 9mm Browning out of my jacket and blown a hole in the ceiling. While he and his crew were gazing at the damage, I stepped forward, smashed his front teeth out with the barrel of the gun and held it in his mouth. 'I am no fucking lady, you piece of shit!' I screamed like a mad bitch ready to shoot the lot of them. Everybody crouched down or hit the floor. Everyone apart from the boss, the middle-man and his brother, that was. 'I want my money back now or I'm going to blow you away, then your mum and dad and all your fucking kids, you ponce!' I screamed. Of course, I wouldn't have hurt his family. But he wasn't to know that.

Blood was pouring out of his mouth and all his hard boys were on the floor, just staring. Their eyes were darting from me, back to their boss and back to me again to me, as if to say, 'What do we do now, boss?' But their boss was just standing there, blood pouring from his mouth. A damp patch appeared on his trousers. He had started to wet himself. I heard a noise behind me.

I whipped out my Mauser while still holding the Browning in this so-called gangster's mouth. I aimed at the noise, keeping my eyes on the boss. When I glanced over, I saw that the disturbance had come from one of his boys – another wannabe gangster crawling from behind the pool table on the brink of tears. 'Just give her back her money. It's not worth it,' he said.

'Get fucking down, you ponce!' I screamed.

It was almost funny. My middle-man had said I was dealing with proper gangsters but here we were, the boss had pissed himself with fear and his boys were crying. So these were the Essex boys, I thought. What a joke. But now I could hear sirens. I told my man to go out and get the car. His brother was now acting like Al Capone, bless him. I didn't blame him. It was like something out of a film and he was loving every minute of this. Everybody was frozen, wanting me to leave before the law arrived. I backed away towards the door, still holding my guns on them as our car pulled up outside. On the way out I said, 'I'm giving you one week – and only one week – to return my money. Yous aren't gangsters. Yous are a load of cardboard cutouts. Proper men don't have people over and they definitely don't cry or piss themselves. You think I'd put my freedom on the line for scum like yous to take away what is mine? I'd die first. One week.'

With that, I was gone. I don't know what they told the coppers when they arrived. If they had any sense, which, to be honest, was asking a lot, they would have been out of there. When we got back home, Matt was waiting. I didn't know how he knew but word must have got out that something had gone down and Matt looked proper worried. In a way, that was when I knew he loved me. I planned to say nothing and act all surprised at him being there, while trying to keep my guns hidden inside my jacket. I knew he would not be happy about what has just gone down.

'What are you doing here, handsome?' I said. I could see he wasn't going to have it but, before I could say anything else, Al Capone blew it for me.

'You should have seen her, Matt. She blew a hole through the ceiling and put them all on the floor. The boss pisses himself. She's knocked his teeth out when she's smashed the gun in his mouth. Then we've done one and she's given them a week to pay or else it's more of the same. They were shitting themselves. I've never seen anything like it, her being a bird an' all.' I gave him a bit of a look at that last bit because I hadn't met a man who was my match yet, apart from the big man standing in front of me.

Al Capone's words hadn't gone down too well with Matt. I knew he still wanted me to be a normal woman. The middle-man was smirking but not for long. 'I can't believe my own ears,' Matt said, grabbing him by the throat, his face contorted with rage. 'What do yous think is funny?' I could see the anger in his face and that was why I had told them not to say anything but Al Capone just hadn't been able to help it.

I started to calm Matt down, pulling him off the middle-man. 'It's not their fault, babe,' I pleaded.

'Don't you get it, Jane? I love you,' he said. 'I'll take care of you from now on and John too. I don't want you to go to work. I don't want you dealing in drugs and I definitely don't want you running around with guns and shooting pubs up.'

But I told him to stop worrying because that was what I did and all I knew. But he was fuming and told the middle-man and his brother to leave us, and they did. By now they couldn't wait to get away from Matt. He had that sort of effect on people.

We started to argue. 'You're not doing no more deals. You're not going to work. I just want to love you!' he screamed. 'You're going to end up dead or doing a life sentence. Please, Jane, let me provide for you. I'll pay you not to work and everything you need, I'll get it for you.'

I loved this man with all my heart by now and he gave me two choices – my old life or him. I so wanted to be cared for and loved by a man who could truly be my everything. My knight in shining armour. No man had ever given me anything. I had always supported myself and I still could. I was always the one who was the provider and it felt like a dream come true for somebody, at last, to have come along and rescued me from this world of crime and villains. It wasn't the money, as I had plenty of that myself because I'd made a small fortune doing the beer run. It was the love, the care and the passion that made me want this man like I'd never wanted any man before. I chose Matt.

Matt moved in and I stopped doing the beer run but I hadn't forgotten about my money. A week went by and I still hadn't had it back. While Matt was at work one day, I went and saw a man who knew the Essex mob. He told me they owned a dry cleaner in Harold Hill but he had now heard about Matt and was more than worried about him. Matt had already warned people that they would have to answer to him if they got me involved in trouble. He said he didn't want to be the one to take me to them but I wasn't interested in listening to his excuses. I told him he was taking me to them. He said Matt would kill him. I just pulled out my Browning, put it to his head and told the poor sod, 'Yeah but I'll kill you first.'

When we got to the dry cleaner, my man begged me to let him go in first to try to sort it out without violence. I agreed. But when he came out, he had a worried look on his face. They had just done a runner out the back door. I wasn't amused. I went in that shop and smashed the place to pieces. I was fuming because I hadn't thought they were total cowards and would do a runner like that. After hiding my guns back in the usual place, I returned home.

When Matt got home, I said, 'I'm going to have to do the Essex mob. It's been a week and I still ain't got my money and they definately ain't getting away with it.' I knew this business wasn't going to end well and I had to tell him what was going to happen, out of respect. That put him in a bad mood straight away.

'No, you're not going to do anyone,' he said. 'You promised not to get into more trouble. I'll sort them out.' I agreed. I owed him that much.

Matt went out that night with a mate and a few hours later he came back with my money. I was over the moon. I thought I'd end up having to do someone but now it was done thanks to him. But at the same time, I knew that being a kept woman didn't work for me. Matt wanted to be with me all the time. The problem was that I found it hard to change overnight, just like that. The more Matt was trying to rein me in, the less I liked it. I could have coped with the love and care he gave me but it was the control I couldn't handle. I had gone from being my own person to him owning me and it wasn't long before things started to change for the worse.

Matt got so controlling that it was unbearable. He stopped all my friends coming over. He didn't like any of them and he kept telling me they weren't my friends and that they didn't really like me. They were just using me, he would say. I was cracking up mentally over it. I wasn't allowed out. I wasn't allowed to have visitors and I felt like he was psychologically destroying me. All he did was put me down. The clothes I wore weren't right, the way I had my hair wasn't right and he said everything and anything he could think of was wrong with me. He did it in such a nice and loving way that I felt he was right. A part of me believed him but the other part of me was fighting it all the way. I really did try to be everything he wanted me to be. He said that he wanted to buy a house in the middle of the forest for me, him and John so that nobody could come near us. Oh, how I tried to be his everything but, in my heart, I knew it wouldn't work. I wanted so badly to stop being a criminal and be the woman Matt wanted but I couldn't. And what's more, I wouldn't. I wouldn't be his prisoner at any price. My heart was breaking.

I worried about my independence and how I would cope if it all ended tomorrow with Matt. So, while I didn't take up the beer run again, I was still doing little deals on puff and Billy without him knowing about it. It wasn't easy. As part of the way he was controlling me, he had said I was too good to do housework and had got one of his mates to do it. This was just his way of keeping an eye on me. I started to resent it because I felt like he was checking up on me in my own home. I went from doing everything for myself to doing nothing apart from a few deals when Matt was out of the house.

He would say, 'All I want you to do is sit there, look gorgeous and do your nails.' But there was more to life than that. And there was more to me. I kept on with my own bits of business, not least because I knew that one day I would return to my old life and would need something to fall back on.

Inevitably, one day he came home early while I was just about to do a little deal. I had to wait for him to fall asleep in the afternoon and then I was off out the door. All the way back I prayed he hadn't woken up. I crept back in but it was too late – he was already out looking for me. I was going to get into bother again when he got back. I had to think fast. When he returned, I told him I'd been at a car-boot fair. I even had some shopping to make it look good but he wasn't stupid. He knew what I'd been up to and went mad, chucking the shopping all over the street and barring me from going out at all.

'What happens to your son when you get blown away or a life sentence?' he raged. 'You don't care, do you?'

To tell you the truth, I never thought about getting shot or caught. I never looked at that possibility. By now I thought I was untouchable – a dangerous way to think but, at that time, that was how I felt. But I also knew that Matt was just trying to possess and control me, which was a completely new experience. The gypsy in me was a wild and free spirit and I just couldn't handle it. It wasn't right and I wasn't having it, no matter what the consequences. It wasn't that Matt wasn't worth it. He was but the word 'compromise' didn't enter either of our heads. I fought against him all the way and the rows got worse.

He kept me indoors for about three months after that incident, saying I couldn't be trusted. I wasn't even allowed to go out to the shops. I was getting really down and couldn't handle it. So I did a runner. I went to the house of a mate who Matt didn't know. I knew Matt would go out looking for me. And anyone who was hiding me would find themselves in trouble too. I was gone for three days before I rang Matt and he pleaded with me to come home. I had to admit I was missing him so, against my better judgment, I decided to return. I phoned a cab, thanked my mate for letting me stay and set off for home. When I reached my house, Matt was waiting outside and I could already see he'd got the right hump. Even as the cab pulled up, I could see he was going to start on me so I told the cab driver, 'Go, go, go! Or this geezer will kill me.' The cab started to take off and Matt started running after us – a sight to put the fear of God into anyone. So the cabby stopped.

I jumped out and Matt ran past me, opened the driver's door and grabbed the driver by the throat. 'Where did you pick her up from?' And the cabby told him. I already knew I was in trouble but now I knew I could have got my mate in the worst trouble of his life. You see, I was learning that nobody went against Matt and got away with it. Hiding his missus from him was bad news for my mate. I was losing it by now. I should have known that Matt wasn't going to let me get away with running away. I was losing my touch. I might have bought a lot of trouble to my mate, although, in the end, it seemed to blow over.

Matt shouted and screamed at me but never hit me. He would never do that because he loved me so much. He had once grabbed me by the hair and I'd hit him over the head with a metal bar. The bar just bounced off him. I'm serious. He was a hard, hard man. He just took a deep breath, shook his head and said, 'That hurt.' But I felt like I had just smashed the bar into a concrete post. I knew it was just as well he loved me too much to hit me as one punch from him would have killed me. The only way to beat him would have been to shoot him and I would never have done that. I loved him and, although he was controlling, I knew it was out of the love he had for me. He would blame others and lash out at them before getting to me, and he was so proud of me. When I got dressed up and we went out to dinner, he loved it but, when the other blokes looked at me, we would start to row, as if it was my fault. He bragged to his mates about how gorgeous I was but it also made him possessive. That was the problem.

Some time later we were off in the Porsche to see some posh people he had done a bit of business with. I got a McDonald's on the way because I was starving. When we were nearly there, he said, 'Jane, don't show me up. Get rid of that Big Mac.' So I chucked it into a bin before I had even finished it. 'And don't talk when we're there. Your voice is so common. Let me do the talking.'

I was shocked. He had made me feel cheap. But I agreed. 'OK, babe. I won't say a word,' I said. But I was fuming. I'd had enough of being controlled by now.

We pulled up and got out of the car and this polite, posh man came over to greet us. He shook Matt's hand and said, 'Hello,' and then he turned to me. 'And who is this gorgeous creature?'

I just looked at him. 'Don't fucking talk to me, you ponce,' I sneered. Nodding at Matt, I added, 'He's just told me I'm not good enough to speak to you so yous had better not speak to me.' It shit him right up.

Who is manipulating who now? I thought. Well, Matt just grabbed me by the hair and dragged me back into the car.

'Shut the fuck up, you mad bitch!' he screamed.

'How did I do?' I asked him, laughing my head off. 'Common enough for you, babe? I think it went very well. I think they were very impressed and we'll definitely be asked round again soon. Don't you, darling?'

He was fuming but so was I. I was always very respectful to people. I treated them how they treated me and I wasn't going to be told I wasn't good enough. Not even by my Matt. He knew he was wrong, in his heart. And he also knew it wasn't in me to be diplomatic. When God made me, he left that bit out. If you want to insult me, you had better be ready for what's coming back because you can be sure that it's definitely coming.

Then one day, early in the morning, the front door came crashing through without any warning. It was the law. Matt and I had been fast asleep. As we laid in bed Matt whispered to me, 'You've got nothing in here, have you? No gear, no guns?'

'No,' I lied.

I had the hand guns and rifles, which I owned legally, and I had my collection of Colt pistols in the safe. Now, they were all fully legal because they were over a hundred years old and classed as antiques. And my bullet-making gear in the safe was also legal because it was made up of legal components. The police were there for about six hours and they didn't find anything at all. But they did, at one point, ask me what was in the safe and, when I told them, 'Guns,' it threw them a bit. I told them I was a collector and they opened the safe and, of course, all the guns were in there. I told them they were all legal but they still took them out and said that, if they were legal, I would get them all back later on. Apart from that, they didn't find anything so we were safe.

When they left, I showed Matt half an ounce of puff I had in my pocket and told him the police were idiots. I was just going to tell him about what was under the shed when he slapped me across the face and went into one, big time. 'You're the fucking idiot,' he said. 'I told you not to do nothing or have anything in the house but, no, you think you're clever. What happens if you'd got caught with that half an ounce? You don't care. Me and John, we'll be left picking up the pieces.' So I didn't tell him about what was under the shed. He was mad enough already. What he doesn't know won't hurt me, I thought.

Sure enough, I got my guns, rifles and bullet-making gear back from the police but I had to go to collect it all from Romford police station. Their arms officer said that my collection was one of the best he had ever seen. I was well impressed with that. I mean, they had seen a lot of weapons and my collection was one of the best. And they still didn't know what was under the garden shed.

By now Matt and I were arguing 24/7 and just hurting each other all the time, even though we loved each other.

It had to come to a head because I had to keep rebelling. It just wouldn't work, mainly because I was too much of a free spirit and I couldn't be what he wanted me to be. I couldn't have my life ruled by a man and I couldn't get away from him because he was too big and strong. I couldn't shoot him because I loved him. But when he was away from me, I missed him so I got myself into a right state. And to make matters worse, him and John had become very close and John really liked him, which, of course, was good. But the rowing was not good for John. And I didn't want my son seeing me unhappy. It just was not right. I was trying to hide it all from John but it was hard.

However, in the end, I'd had enough of him controlling me and despite everything I'd thought through so many times, I pulled a gun on him. 'Get out now, Matt,' I told him. 'This is no good for either of us and it's no good for John. I won't let us destroy him.'

Now, say what you want about Matt but he loved my boy like his own and those words sank in. He walked away when I said that. And, let's be honest, even a bird with a gun couldn't have made Matt do that if he didn't want to. So he did do the right thing. But it wasn't to last.

A couple of weeks later I was driving to buy a bit of puff in Kent. Matt happened to see me on the road and started to come after me in one of the many cars he owned. I put my foot down but he caught me easily, cutting me up and heading me off. He got out of the car, punched in the windows of my van with his bare hands and dragged me through the window. Cars were slowing down and people were watching. He was trying to put me in the boot of his motor but I fought him all the way. Two cars crashed because they were watching us. A police van pulled up and two coppers got out and started to come over. I was screaming for help but Matt just shouted that it was a domestic and put me in the boot. They didn't lift a finger. I couldn't believe it. Then he drove off in his car with my van abandoned on a roundabout near Ashford, in Kent, with a smashed window and the engine still running. He took me to a house I had never seen before – one of his safe houses, I guessed. I was basically under house arrest by Matt and his mates. A right old state of affairs.

He went back to get the van and I knew he might find I had a squirter (a plastic bottle with ammonia to squeeze in a fight), a knuckle duster and a joint in the glove box. The only thing out of that lot that would worry him was the joint. Drugs were a big no-no with Matt, unless it came to selling them. I wasn't even allowed to smoke fags in front of him, let alone a joint so I would be in big trouble when he found it. But by the time he got back to the van the two coppers had called for back-up and he was quickly arrested for the knuckle duster, squirter and joint in the glove box. Not good!

His mate came back and told me he'd been nicked and taken to Ashford station. I told the mate to take me to the police station. I might not have been getting on with

Matt at that moment but I wasn't about to let him take the fall for me. So off we went. I was arrested and they let Matt out. They asked me why I'd had the weapons and I told them I was going to use them to do Matt.

'You what?'

'Yeah but he won't be bothered about that,' I said. 'We've got a love-hate relationship. It's the joint he's going to kill me for. He is very disapproving of drugs.' I actually wanted them to arrest me and put me in a cell to keep Matt off me. I was scared about what he might do now. Things had got out of hand, to say the least. 'Just keep me in here,' I pleaded. 'I'm guilty – they are my weapons, it's my joint so just lock me up.' To my horror, they chucked me out of the station after giving me a good talking to. They said how grateful I should be to have a man who was prepared to take me on. They thought I was madder than Matt. I got the big speech about how Matt was a decent, hard-working man who was trying to do the best by me and how I was an ungrateful woman. Well, I could see Matt had charmed the coppers around, just like he did everyone else. I didn't have a chance. I was an unmarried mother from the East End with drugs and weapons so they took his side. They forgot all about him putting me in the boot of his car. But I suppose me telling them I was going to do Matt with the weapons didn't help my case!

Matt was waiting for me when I got out and I was bang in trouble. I knew that he was not amused. He took me back to the safe house, where we rowed all night long. 'I've got money. All you have to do is look beautiful. That's all I want, Janie. Is that so hard? Most women would kill to be in your position,' he kept saying. And he was right. They would. But I couldn't handle it. I couldn't allow myself to be controlled or imprisoned by anyone. But love is the strongest drug of all. I agreed to his terms and promised I'd go back and stay with him and not get up to anything. But I knew, even as I said it, I was lying. I loved him so much but I knew I couldn't keep my promise. All we were doing now was hurting each other.

I was also starting to get paranoid that Matt would take John away from me, as they were really close and, every time me and Matt had a break-up, he said he was going to take John. I was so worried that I told my boy that, if he went with Matt, he would lose all his mates and Matt would lock him up in a room. John was only 11 at the time and, if I'm honest, I was a bit jealous of their friendship. They got on so well. I hadn't realised how much I'd worried John with talk of Matt taking him until one day when he was out with his mates at the local video shop. He rang me to say there were two blokes watching him from their Ford Escort van.

'How many of you are there, John?' I asked.

'There's about twenty of us, Mum,' he said.

'Don't worry, babe, you're all right. There are too many of yous for anyone to try anything.' Poor John. I'd convinced him Matt was going to kidnap him but, in my heart, I didn't think it would come to that. But then

John called me back. The two blokes were Irish and I started worrying because Matt had told me he'd have two of his Irish boys take John to Ireland and that I'd never see him again. So, when I heard the word 'Irish' from John, I panicked. 'I'm on my way,' I said.

I grabbed my samurai sword, jumped in my van and flew round to the video shop. I could see the van with the two blokes in it and all the kids were outside the shop. I pulled across the front of the van and blocked them in. I jumped out with my sword and asked John, 'Are these them?' He said, "Yes," and, straight away, I went for the door but the blokes knew they were in trouble. They had already locked the doors. They could see me with a big shiny sword – hardly a common sight – and they were panicking. I'd gone into Gran mode. No one was taking my boy.

I lifted the sword above my head, two-handed, and smashed it as hard as I could into the windscreen. It cracked and shattered but didn't cave in so I started smashing the van as hard and as many times as I could. I wanted to get at these blokes. They knew now that, if I got to them, they would be in mortal danger but they couldn't drive away as my van was blocking them in. So, in a blind panic, they ground the gears, dropped the clutch and lurched straight at me. They were trying to run me over. The van mounted the pavement, I jumped out of the way and, wheels spinning and gears crunching, they sped off. I had smashed their van to pieces and, when they reached a safe distance, they stopped and one of them got out. 'You're a fucking nutter!' he shouted. 'We're calling the police.'

Now, I had my sword gripped in both hands out in front of me and I shouted back, 'You're scaring the kids! Don't scare the kids!' They drove off.

I looked round and there must have been a couple of hundred people watching me. They were probably thinking I was scaring the kids more than the men in the van were, which was a fair point. It certainly looked like I was scaring them. I had my Gran face on and I'd got a big sword held in both hands like I was ready to chop someone up, samurai-style. They must have been thinking it was like something out of *Kill Bill*. All I needed was a yellow leather catsuit and it would have been. But, fortunately, no violence was required. I just told John to get in the van and we went home for a cup of tea. The incident was the talk of Rainham for a while.

Matt phoned up later that day saying he had heard about what had happened and wanted to make sure me and John were OK.

I was fuming. 'Don't give me, "Am I OK?"' I said. 'You've sent two of your soldiers round to take my John. Well, they came proper unstuck, didn't they?'

'What are you on about, you stupid cow?' he said. 'I wouldn't do that to you.'

'Oh, fuck off,' I said. That was the end of me and Matt. There was no going back now. He had frightened my boy by sending those men but it had backfired on him. I would have killed them if I had got into their van and Matt now knew it. Using my son to get at me was a no-go area. He had just crossed the line, big time. John and I were OK together. We had each other and that was what mattered the most. Matt was well and truly gone.

It was sad for me at first though. Despite everything, I really loved Matt and my heart was broken. I had more money than I could count from all the beer runs. There were more people around me than I needed, yet I was the unhappiest and loneliest person in the room. You see, everybody was your mate when you had everything, which, at that time, I did. But Matt and I were finished. I was all smiles on the outside, for the world, but in my heart and soul I was sobbing like a baby. Well, this is what you wanted, girl, I told myself. So get a grip and get back to what you do best. I had my John and I didn't need anyone else. As long as John was OK, I was OK. And John was, as always, the perfect son.

Life went on.

8

GUNNED DOWN

I am not to question why,
I am but to do or die.

Someone from the beer run asked me one day if I wanted to do a robbery.

'Why not?' I said. 'I've not earned for a while and, anyway, I'm bored.'

The job sounded easy. It was all set up. I was going to stick up a delivery man who had £80,000 in cash in a bag. It was tax-evasion money from a big player who was supplying booze from the continent to off-licences. The delivery man was in on it and that was what made it so easy. The cash couldn't go in the bank because it could have been traced, so it was to be transferred from the off-licence to a house for safekeeping. I was going to hold them up with two others while the delivery man was on the way but, since all he had to do was act like he was being robbed, it was going to be a piece of cake.

The day before the job, the two blokes who told me about it decided they didn't fancy it. They thought it was too risky. I couldn't believe it. 'It's a piece of piss,' I said. 'What is wrong with you? What can go wrong?' But they didn't change their minds. They said that, even though it looked easy, it was a bit out of their league.

They'd had a look at my arsenal of weapons and said, 'You're fucking crazy, woman.'

I was still going through with it. The next day I got my guns – a Colt .38 and a replica Browning pistol. The replica was to point at the bag man because he said he didn't want a loaded gun pointed at him, which was fair enough. Just in case he was being watched by possible witnesses, it would then look as if he really was being robbed. I planned to have the real gun ready in case the owners of the cash showed up and decided to get brave.

The day of the job was a Sunday. I did my boy's dinner, put on my full combat gear and got Tracey to watch John, as he was mates with her own boy. I planned to be home by 9pm and they waved me goodbye as I drove off on the job.

The transfer was at 7 pm and I waited in my van outside Valentines Park in Gants Hill, near Ilford, where I could see both the off-licence and the house the money was being taken to. I was sitting in a white Ford Transit, which belonged to the man who had supplied me with the information. I loaded my Colt .38, just in case. At length, I saw the runner come from the off-licence with the satchel over his shoulder, just as I was told he would. I drove almost level with him, pulled out the replica Browning, waited for him to walk past my open window and pointed the gun in his face. 'Give me the satchel, mate,' I said nicely. But something was wrong. I could see it in his face from the off.

To my disbelief he said, 'No.'

'Give me the fucking money,' I said again through gritted teeth. 'What are you fucking playing at?' He didn't answer but just started to run. I was not amused with what was happening. I began to see it was a set-up. Now I knew why the other two didn't come. My target was now legging it down the road. This was not on at all and I cursed myself under my breath for not twigging when the other two pulled out at the last minute. To make matters worse, the runner had got some balls. I mean, most people would have handed over the cash but he had done his job. I threw the imitation gun on the passenger seat and grabbed the Colt .38 but by this time my man was among a group of people. There were two families on the opposite side of the road coming out of the houses and getting into their cars, and quite a few pedestrians up ahead where the runner was headed. This was a crowded street. I spun the van around and, my gun in my hand, I shouted at everyone, 'Get down, get down!' They thought I was going to shoot them but I just wanted the runner and to warn them. It was all going pear-shaped big time because no one had noticed him. They all looked at me before hitting the ground – all apart from the runner who was still trying to get away. He was hiding behind those people who were too far to have dropped down yet and I just couldn't believe what was happening. This wasn't the plan. I was waving a gun at a crowded street and I knew I was in big trouble but it was about to get a lot, lot worse.

Satchel-boy knew I wanted to do him and he ran behind a woman. There was a look of pure terror in her eyes and she started screaming. That set a few others off and then I could hear police sirens. Soon, out of the corner of my eye, I saw a police car. I'd got a whole street on the ground at gunpoint and I had to get out of this situation. I threw the gun in the back of the van, put my foot down and drove off as fast as I could. I was driving the van at up to 70 mph as though it was a mini. But at every turn I could see police cars. Then I heard a helicopter above me and it seemed as though the whole of Scotland Yard was after me. But I didn't give up.

Soon I could see the helicopter clearly. It was hovering in front of me, flying backwards but the pilot was looking straight at me. This close it looked like something from outer space. All I could really see was a big glass dome with men in it, helmets over their faces, big goggles over their eyes. A spotlight was shining down on me. 'Shit, shit, shit!' I screamed. I had a high-powered torch in the van, which I grabbed and pointed directly at the helicopter. The beam was so powerful it dazzled the pilot and suddenly the helicopter banked and turned away from me to avoid crashing onto the busy street below. He did the right thing because I wasn't going down without a fight.

I was screeching down turnings at random and before long I flew down a dead-end road. There was a brick wall in front of me and, behind me, a sea of police cars. But there had been a turning to my left, just behind me, so I stuck the van into reverse, smashed into a police car, forcing it out of the way, and spun the van round in the direction of the turning. 'I've got to get out of this,' I said to myself. 'I've told my boy I'll be home at nine.'

I was just about to put my foot down and head into the turn leading to a clear road when an armed officer, aiming an M16 rifle straight at me, shouted through the driver's window, 'Armed police. Show me your hands!' He had appeared from nowhere. He was standing by the side of the van. I hadn't seen him jump out of the car I had rammed into. The barrel of his gun was inches from my head. Time stood still. I stared straight back at him through the window. It's now or never, I thought, my eyes darting from him to the turning in the road. I was as calm as you like. Then, for some reason, words that I had lived by came into my head and told me what to do – Mine is not to question why, I am but to do or die. That had always been my mantra when I was in danger. My gypsy blood would never allow me to go down without a fight.

I laughed in the copper's face. 'Yeah, really?' The red

dot of his laser sight was flicking around my face. He
wasn't expecting those words. I supposed I was meant to
shit myself and crumble. It didn't happen. For a long
moment the copper was motionless. I knew now that, if
I didn't get away, I'd get it in the head. I laughed again
and then smashed my foot down on the accelerator and
the van lurched, then roared forward. But the turn was
too tight and I lost control and crashed the van into a
house on the corner. In the mayhem I didn't hear
anything but the copper I had taunted had his M16 set
on semi-automatic and fired off four shots. I could see
my hands covered in blood and the windscreen was a
red mist. My blood. I'd been shot. Then the van door
was pulled open and I could hear the cops screaming at
me. They were going mental. I mean mental. 'Armed
police. Armed police. Show us your hands. Show us
your hands!'

I was dragged out of the van and handcuffed. Now I
was laughing at them. They tried to spread me star-
shaped on the ground but my hands were cuffed above
my head. I looked up at them all and laughed again.
'You load of fucking pigs,' I said. But before I could
finish, six guns came down into my face.

'Shut your fucking mouth or we'll blow your fucking
head off,' one of them said. There were loads of them,
all in full body armour. I was in no doubt that, if I made
one false move, I would have been taken out. Another
one of the cops stood on my hands and, for the first
time, I realised I had been shot in the right hand. I

stopped laughing as the adrenalin started to wear off. I didn't know it yet but in all I'd been shot four times. I knew I was facing serious time and I thought about my boy at home. If I realised how badly I'd been hurt, I would have wondered if I was dying. The first bullet had entered my right forearm and ripped its way down to lodge in my hand. The second had gone into the back of my right shoulder and exited through the front of the same shoulder. The third had entered my back, behind my heart, and the last had ricocheted off the dashboard and got me in the groin. Just my luck. But I still didn't feel a thing. I knew I'd been shot in the hand because I could see a big hole in it but I hadn't got a clue about the other wounds.

The armed police were screaming at everyone coming out of their houses to stay away. I was lying in a pool of my own blood in Royal Close, Ilford, wondering what the hell had happened. I found out later that the police officer opened fire because he thought I was going to run him over. That was what I was told but all the shots came from behind me as I tried to get away. I had been shot in the back, driving away, so how could I have been trying to run him over?

But maybe I was dying. All of a sudden my dad was there cradling and rocking me and telling me I was going to be OK. I could hear him shouting, 'Get these cuffs off her. She's been hit everywhere. There's blood coming out of her everywhere. We're going to lose her. Stay with me, babe. You're going to be OK. I've got you.'

'I'm OK, Dad,' I replied. And that was the last thing I remembered. I passed out. But the man holding me wasn't my dad. He was an ordinary police officer. Not one of the armed ones. This copper picked me up, got the cuffs off me and held me as if I was a baby until the ambulance got there. I'd like to thank him for that, whoever he is.

I woke up in the King George hospital, Ilford, with two police officers in my room. All I could think was that my dad was going to go mad and Matt was going to kill me because he had warned me not to get involved with the villains who had given me the information. He had told me they were wrong 'uns and, as usual, I hadn't believed him. I thought he was just saying that so I didn't do any more jobs but he was right again. I had now been shot four times and was looking at a life sentence.

I lay in the hospital bed recovering from the blood transfusion I'd had to replace all the blood I lost. I'd had two operations to remove three bullets that had lodged in my body. The bullet that blew a hole in my hand and the two that went into my back and groin had to be removed in the operating theatre. In all, I needed more than 350 stitches to keep me together. It wasn't only bullets they took out of me. It was the bits of van metal propelled by the bullets into my body. I had other splinters from the van in me as well. I mean, I had half the bleedin' van in me. I'd been flung into the windscreen and had to have chunks of glass removed from my arms. Some of the debris was buried so deep that they had to pick shrapnel out of my arms and back for about ten months. I didn't even know about much of it until it worked its way to the surface. Then they would dig it out.

I was on the critical but stable list but, when I woke up, it was as though nothing had happened. I couldn't feel any pain anywhere. It was unbelievable. Then in walked my dad and John and I grabbed hold of my boy. He was only 12 and I could see he'd been crying but, when he saw me and realised I was OK, his face lit up. Believe it or not, we all started laughing.

The doctors told me I should have died but I told them it takes more than four bullets to keep me down. I don't feel any different from any other day. My boy was OK and, as long as he was OK, I felt like nothing could hurt me. According to Dad, the police said I'd been shooting at them and that's why they opened fire. I told Dad I didn't shoot at anyone and that, if it had been me firing four shots, I would have got four coppers in their heads.

'Shush, Jane. Don't talk like that,' my dad said under his breath. 'The place is crawling with the old bill and you're in enough trouble as it is.' Of course, he was right so I toned it down. And it was just bravado anyway. I felt so guilty because of my boy. He deserved better.

The cops questioned me while I was in bed and I told them I hadn't done anything wrong. 'A man tried to rape me, then he tried to hurt a load of people in the street,' I said. 'I tried to help them and I'm the one who gets shot, just for saving myself.' Even the cops had to hide the smirks on their faces. They should have given me an Oscar for that one! But you've got to try something. After all, I had put a whole street of people on the ground at gunpoint and the runner was saying I had tried to rob him. I was looking at life for armed robbery and it was easily possible I would be charged with attempted murder of police officers because they were saying I shot at them. Now I knew I had done wrong. But I wasn't guilty of attempted murder.

I told Dad and John not to worry because I didn't believe God would save me from four bullets to give me a life sentence for something I didn't do. I told them that everything would be OK and put them all at ease. I think they left the hospital happier than they were when they arrived. But God only knows what they must have been thinking. Their hearts must have been breaking, seeing me like that.

I was told I was going to be transferred to a burns unit at Basildon University hospital for plastic surgery on my hand, which was in a bad way. I arrived the next day and, while I was in my room, I could hear a commotion outside and then Matt burst in. He looked really worried. But he was angry too. 'What's happened?' he asked, looking at my hand and all the tubes and drips I was linked to. So I started with the whole story. Before I could say anything to stop him he reacted by going mad and he began throwing police officers down the corridor.

'You shot my missus!' he screamed and the police were terrified. He was a very powerful man and had brought a firm with him. Believe me, they made their presence known. I think the cops must have thought Matt was going to try to spring me from the hospital or something because they had called in the army to guard me. There were police and soldiers on the roof, in the corridors, right outside my room. There must have been 20 in the corridor alone. Police dogs patrolled outside and they had put security checks in place a mile around the hospital. If you came to the hospital, you were treated like a terrorist, partly because I was a dangerous criminal and partly because they reckoned Matt was planning an escape for me.

But a couple of days later I got a message saying Matt had been shot. I couldn't believe it. I had a feeling he had gone after the geezers who grassed me up. At least he was only hit in the shoulder and he was OK. I didn't get to see him for a while but he sent me the biggest bunch of flowers I've ever seen and I knew he was OK.

After being in hospital for ten days I was told I could leave. I think they were relieved to get rid of me. I mean, this was a hospital and it looked like a prisoner-of-war camp with soldiers patrolling the place. I was taken to East Ham police station and they put me in a cell with no toilet paper and a blocked bog. I wasn't amused. I mean, I'd just got out of hospital and had three bullets taken out of me and one of them was in the groin. This place was unhygienic. But I was a soldier, I told myself, and crashed out on the bunk.

The next day they took me to be interviewed and believe me when I say I had two of their best interviewing me. I mean, these were the best of the best. They offered me a fag and asked me what I was doing waving a gun about and threatening people. So I said, 'It was like this, officers. I went to test the guns I'd restored in the park. I know I shouldn't have. But I was curious to see if they fired OK. Being close to bonfire night, I thought no one would take any notice and just think the sounds were fireworks.'

'But you had an imitation gun as well. What was that for?'

I said, 'Oh, that one's for my boy for Christmas. I was going to have a little go with that as well.'

'But where did you get the bullets from?'

'I made them,' I said. I told them I was a restorer of antique guns. I thought I was doing OK.

'Why did you hold up a man at gunpoint and force a whole street on the ground in fear of their lives then?'

'I never held a man up at gunpoint. I asked this man for directions to Gants Hill and he said, "Let me get in and I'll show you the way." I said, "No way, mate, you can't get in," and started to drive off when he went for his satchel and said, "I've got something to show you." I thought he was going for a knife or gun so I picked up my gun and said, "I've got something to show you," and he runs into a group of people and I think, Oh, no, he's a nutter and he's going to hurt somebody. I tried to help them. I was shouting at them to be careful when I realised I've still got the gun in my hand and they are more scared of me than they are of him.'

Well, there was a bit of a silence. Then one of them took a deep breath. 'Let me get this right,' he said. 'You not only saved yourself but you saved the whole street as well?'

'Yes,' I said.

'Well, we put it to you that you went to rob this man and you tried to involve two innocent people but they decided not go with you when they saw your weapons,' he said, 'They told you they don't mind doing a burglary but that they think you're mad and out of their league.' Well, well, well, I thought. Now I knew I was definitely set up and grassed. I should have known when the two men said they weren't coming with me but now I knew for sure. But I didn't say a word of that to the cops.

'Don't be silly,' I said. 'You've been listening to Jack, haven't you?'

'Jack who?' the chatty one asked.

'*Jackanory*,' I said. I couldn't believe what had happened. Professional villains, in my opinion, should have more self-respect than to behave in the way that those two had. It was obvious the police knew exactly what had gone off but they still had to prove it. They tried a different approach.

'Our armed response team have told us you tried to kill two of them.'

This wasn't funny anymore.

'I can't believe that one. Are yous being serious?' I asked. 'You shot me four times, remember? I didn't shoot anyone.'

'You were only shot because you tried to shoot two officers.'

'Look. I never fired a shot. I know I rammed them but, believe me, they were in my blind spot behind the van and I didn't see them there.'

They said the officer who shot me was standing in front of the van and I tried to run him and another officer down and that's why he shot me.

'What a load of crap. He was to the side of me and there was no second officer. I only wanted to get away from him, not kill him,' I told them.

Their story was changing. At first, the officers had said I'd been shooting and that was why they shot me. Now they were saying I tried to run two officers down. I knew that, in time, forensics would prove I hadn't fired a shot and I guessed they already knew that and that was why they were trying this new angle.

'Well, we've got a vicar and his son who witnessed it and they swear on the bible that one officer was in front of you,' the copper said. 'And the vicar and his son said you were screaming with laughter and drove right at the officer and he had no other choice but to fire or he would be dead. These are men of God. They wouldn't lie now, would they?'

Only God could know what the police told the vicar

I'd done but I would have sworn by the bible myself that I was telling the truth. I didn't try to hurt anybody apart from the runner that didn't play the way he was supposed to. It wasn't looking good though. I'd got the vicar and his son against me, police officers, the runner, a street full of people and the witnesses who saw me driving like a maniac. But I told the two coppers what I thought. 'God didn't save me from four bullets so yous can fit me up and life me off,' I said. 'God's on my side. I haven't done nothing wrong. I know I shouldn't have took my guns out to test but I've got four bullets in me for that. God won't let yous stitch me up. He's on my side.'

'So where did you get the van?' one of them asked.

'I hired it.' I told them it came from a mate but that I couldn't really remember the exact details. I didn't want to involve anyone else.

The senior one of the two said, 'Oh, well, you may not remember them but the firm you hired the van from remembers you very well. In fact, let me read you this statement: "I remember the women very well. She was dressed head to toe in full combat gear. She was so eager to hire the van that I charged her twice the usual rate and, when I asked if she wanted me to show her how to drive the van, she said no and sped off like lightning."'

I told the coppers I didn't know what they were talking about. They charged me with possession of firearms and ammunition, attempted armed robbery, the attempted murder of two police officers and dangerous driving. I was looking at life.

By now they were not being as nice as they were when I'd gone into the interview room. In fact, they were being nasty. They packed me off to my cell. Sitting on my own once more, I couldn't believe how people could go so dodgy on me. One word from me and I could have had all those who had betrayed me and grassed me up behind bars, just like I was. But I was not scum like them. Whether I got out of this or not, I said to myself, I could hold my head high because I wasn't a grass.

PART TWO

PRISON

9

BANGED UP —
HER MAJESTY'S PRISON
HOLLOWAY

*In the eyes of the law, I was the most
dangerous woman in Britain.*

The papers were full of it.

COPS SHOOT GUN GIRL, screamed the *Sun*. BLONDE
FIRED TWO GUNS AT US — SO WE SHOT HER DOWN, said the
Daily Mirror. Even *The Times* got in on the act: POLICE
MARKSMAN SHOOTS ARMED WOMAN AFTER ROBBERY BID.
And the *News of the World* couldn't resist the story
under the headline: COPS SHOOT GUN WOMAN AFTER
CHASE. The *People* did a huge double-page spread about
the police armed response unit that captured me. NO
TIME TO RUN, NO PLACE TO HIDE, JACK DROPS HIS MP5 TO
HIS HIP AND LETS RIP AT THE DRUG-MAD BLONDE TRYING TO
MOW HIM DOWN.

Blimey, I thought to myself. Some of the reporting was
accurate but some of it wasn't. But, whichever way you

read it, I was Britain's most dangerous female criminal and the tabloids lapped it up. I was famous for all the wrong reasons but now I need to set the record straight on a couple of things the press had to say about me. The *People* described me as a 'drug dealer with a dangerous addiction'. 'She needed the money to finance her dealing,' it went on and said I was 'high on drugs' when I went on the job. That piece, which came out a couple of years after the shooting, described me as a 'drug-mad blonde'.

The article was publicising a book called *The Trojan Files*, which told the story of London's armed response units and the procedure under which I was arrested – Operation Trojan. It was written by Sergeant Roger Gray, who has since left Scotland Yard. They made me sound like a heroin and crack addict, the cheeky sods. I've never taken heroin or crack in my life. I hate that shit. The book showed a reconstruction of the police marksman capturing me and, although the write-up was blown well out of proportion, the reconstruction photo was brilliant. They had used a really pretty blonde girl who looked a lot like me and I was well chuffed with that. It was the text that was wrong. I didn't have a 'deadly addiction'. I had done a little bit of Billy to keep me alert but no way was I high. I was too professional to go on a job in that state. And anyway, as I've said, my limit was a bit of puff to relax and I only really used speed when I was on the beer run to keep me going. But the reports did help me understand how much mayhem I caused that night.

The police units that came after me were from Operation Trojan's specialist armed response units and by the time the first armed unit got to Ilford I was already being followed by eight local patrol cars as well as the Trojan mob. When I was arrested, there were over 50 officers at the scene. It was the first time that any armed police response unit had been involved in shooting a woman.

The Times quoted the 15-year-old schoolboy son of the vicar. This was the boy the cops had told me about. He said he saw an officer fire through my windscreen when it looked as if he might be mown down as I attempted to turn the van out of the cul-de-sac to get away. The boy said, 'The van was revving up and the wheels were turning, then suddenly a police officer standing there just shot. I think he thought the van was going to run him over. I heard four shots in quick succession and I ran back in because I did not want to get caught in gunfire.' I didn't understand why that boy had said what he'd said because I never tried to run anyone over – rather, I only wanted to escape. He was later proved to be wrong by forensics and all I can say is thank God for forensics because my word wouldn't have counted for anything against those of a vicar's son and the police.

They took me from East Ham police station to court and I was remanded in custody and carted off under armed guard to London's Holloway prison for women. I was designated a category-A prisoner, meaning I was one of the most dangerous inmates in the land and likely to attempt escape. Cat A meant I was bang in trouble from the start. I was segregated and had no communication with any other prisoners but, as I hadn't ever been in prison before, I thought this was what everyone got. I didn't know that I was the only Cat A prisoner in Holloway when I arrived. I still thought of myself primarily as a mum trying to do her best for her boy but, the way I was treated when I arrived, you would think I was more dangerous than Bonnie and Clyde put together. I still had about 350 stitches in me and, generally, I looked like I'd just got back from a war with the amount of holes and wounds I'd got.

Just 12 days after I was shot I was in Holloway on C1 wing. This was the nutters' wing where all the Broadmoor cases were but I didn't know that at the time. To me, they were just ordinary prisoners. The officers took me to my cell and I didn't see one prisoner on the way because the prison was on lockdown. I didn't even know that this was because of me. I didn't know what Cat A meant at that precise moment. I just thought this was all normal as it was my first time inside. I was accompanied by 20 red-and-black screws. The heavy mob – specialist officers whose role was to act as security over and above ordinary screws. They got their name from the red badges they wear on black uniforms and they were only called in when there was trouble, such as a riot or a fight. Ordinary screws, hundreds of them, lined the corridors as the heavy mob walked me to my cell. I'd been strip searched on entering the prison and the cell we reached at the end of it all looked fucking grim.

It had a lump of concrete, like a long shelf or slab, built out from the wall, with a pillow and grey blankets that looked like they had come from World War II. That was my bed. There was a cardboard table and chair and a bible. Next to the 'bed' was a toilet and sink with a towel in the corner. This cell was eight feet long by six feet wide. There wasn't enough room to swing a cat. Once I was in I was strip searched again. They took all my bandages off and I complained straight away. 'You aren't allowed to do that,' I said. 'The hospital have been checking my wounds several times a day because I've had plastic surgery and have been warned about getting it infected.' I'd had skin grafted onto my hand from the top of my legs.

'You're not in hospital now,' one of the screws said. 'You are not going to try to strangle any of us with your bandages,' and, sure enough, off they came. The screws left me there like that, with just my thoughts for company.

My wounds looked bad so I wrapped my arm in the rough old prison towel. Then in came the doctor with some pills but, before he was allowed in my cell, I had to be strip searched again. Then he was let in under full guard. I was on about eight different tablets from the hospital but he said I was not allowed some because they weren't in prison regulations. So he gave me some medicine of his own that was an orange colour and a tub of white cream for my skin. He said I had to take the medication in front of him, which I did, and then he left and I was strip searched again. I swear to God that there were about ten or fifteen of the heavy mob that had not left my side. Now I was finding out what Cat A meant and, because I was Cat A, the Governor had to come to check on me every day. I realised I was a top-security prisoner when the Governor didn't even enter my cell but only opened the hatch from the outside. I had to stand up and walk over to the door. The first time he came, he asked if I had any problems.

'No, I feel good,' I said. Well, he just shut the hatch and walked off and I giggled to myself. This became one of my stock answers every time any officers or the Governor came to my cell. I would always make out I was fine. Sometimes I would start dancing in my cell and singing, 'I feel good, I knew that I would.' They used to say I was nutty. I did this because I'd never let them know I was down. It was my way of staying strong.

But I was missing my boy like you wouldn't imagine. John had turned 12 now. All his life he'd had me there and now he was alone in that big dangerous world. He was with my mum and dad but they didn't really know him. Not to put too fine a point on it, when I'd lived with them when I was 12, things hadn't been too clever. But I had to block that thought out of my mind and I prayed to God, 'Please let John get through this, God. Please. You can do anything to me. I'll take it on the chin. I won't be offended with whatever you decide to let happen to me. I know I deserve it but please watch over my son.'

My dad and my sister Shell would be looking after John. Shell lived opposite my parents with her husband and three boys. Kevin, Shell's middle son, and John were only six weeks apart in age and were more like brothers than cousins. John would survive, I told myself. Yet it was going to be hard because I knew Matt had been shot so he couldn't be around for my boy.

Most people get off on other people's misery and, when things in your life are looking a bit bleak, they thrive on it. But I wasn't going to give anybody the pleasure or the opportunity to thrive off me and mine. And if they thought four bullets and what looked like a life sentence were going to wipe the smile off my face, well, they didn't know me. I didn't think so, somehow. Would you think so? So while anybody was near, I didn't show a flicker of emotion. It wasn't going to happen. When I was lying in bed alone, that was the time to grieve. But to the outside world, I was always happy and nothing they could do would change that.

I was only allowed a bible in my cell on C wing and I tried to read it. But I couldn't concentrate because the girl in the cell next to me was shouting all the time. 'Gi's a fag, gi's a fag.' All day long. When the heavy mob checked on me, I asked them to give her a fag.

'It's hard enough being locked up in a cell 24/7, let alone without a fag,' I said. They explained that she kept burning herself. But she wouldn't stop screaming, 'Gi's a fag! Gi's a fag!'

So I shouted that I'd tried to get her a fag but the screws wouldn't allow it. 'I don't fucking want a fag off you anyway,' she called.

'You fucking ungrateful cow.'

'I'll do you if I get the chance.'

But when, at last, we got to talking properly, I found I liked her. There was a glass slit in the door, which was about an inch wide and six inches long, and through it I could see the girl. She was in the cell opposite mine and I swear to God she looked as normal as anybody else. We talked all the time until one day I could hear a noise coming from her cell and I looked over to see that she was covered in blood from head to toe. She had broken her phone card in half and was slicing herself to pieces with it. There was blood everywhere.

'No!' I screamed. 'Stop!'

I felt for this woman. She had lost her kids through coming to prison and she wasn't handling it too well. Who could blame her? Anyway, the screws and heavy mob burst into her cell, all in riot gear with helmets and shields as big as they were. They put her in a straitjacket and took everything out of her cell and threw her back in it with just the straitjacket on until the doctor arrived. He took the jacket off, cleaned up her wounds and then the screws put her back in the jacket. My heart went out to her. She was crying for help and needed to be in hospital, not a stinking cell.

As for me, I had been inside a week and still hadn't even been allowed a bath or a visit. I really was beginning to understand what being Cat A meant. It was the attempted-murder charge that had done it. Believe me, trying to kill a copper is the worst crime to be accused of in Britain – even actually killing one is not that much worse. On paper, it looked like I had wanted to do it but not succeeded. In their eyes, there was little difference. I mean, the police who were there should have known it was a load of old rubbish. I was doing wrong and I was up to villainy, yes, but I did not have murder on my mind and I did not try to do murders. I did not pull the trigger. I knew I was in trouble because, if I was found not guilty, the police would have lost their justification for shooting at me.

In the meantime, in the eyes of the law, I was the most dangerous woman in Britain, which meant visitors had to be vetted at the nearest police station before they were allowed anywhere near me in prison. My dad, John and my mum all came to see me as the weeks went by. My dad was my first visitor. He wanted to come sooner than a week but they wouldn't let him. When he came, they put the prison on lockdown and I was strip searched yet again before being taken to the visitor's wing by the heavy mob. Throughout the visit they stood there, two of them on either side of him and two on either side of me. Watching and listening to every private word. There was also a glass screen between me and Dad.

'You all right, my girl?' were my dad's first words, concern written all over his face.

'I'm having the time of my life in here, Dad,' I told him, pressing against the glass where his hand was, more worried for him than I was for myself. 'There is a swimming pool, disco every night and it's just pure fun. It's a holiday camp, Dad.'

A big smile covered his face, the colour came back into cheeks and I could see a weight lifted from his shoulders. He was always going to worry about me but at least he knew now I was mentally strong. Of course, I didn't tell him what it was really like but Dad knew that already from his own years behind bars. I was coping. That was all he needed to know and that was what I told him. And it was true. I reminded him of his own words to me as a kid. 'Remember what you told me as a little girl, Dad?' I asked. 'Tough times don't last but tough people do.' When he left, he had the twinkle back in his eyes and the smile back on his face, even though I swear there was a little tear in his eye, which he tried to hide from me.

His final words were, 'I'm proud of you, Jane, how you're handling it. We are all here for you, girl.'

I was putting Dad through hell but he put his own feelings aside and was only thinking of me and how he could help. There were tears in my eyes too that day. I was proud of him. He was the quiet but silent type and, when I needed him, he was there. 'I love you so much, Dad,' I said as he got up to go. I wanted to hug him so much but there was no way through that glass screen.

On the way back to my cell I was strip searched yet again and by now it was beginning to piss me off, big time. 'Do you think I'm a fucking magician and my dad's conjured up a gun out of thin air?' I said. The screws could sense my mood was turning nasty because they were ruining the nice feelings I had from seeing Dad.

'It's the rules,' one said.

'Look. I've just seen my dad and I'm not letting you ruin it with another strip search,' I said. 'You know I haven't got nothing on me so, if you want it, bring it on if you're brave enough but I am not being strip searched again.' I knew they would have battered me but I would have done a couple of them first, as you will find out later on, but not this time. They let me back in my cell without another search.

Soon it wasn't just my dad visiting me. Matt and John came. My defence lawyer, Gary Jacobs, started to visit too. He warned that the charges against me were very serious and that I could be looking at life or years behind bars in double figures. But I told him I was innocent of all the charges and that he had to find a way to prove that. Gradually, as we went through the details over several visits, I could see he was starting to believe me on the attempted murder charges but proving it was another matter. He knew it wouldn't be easy because the police needed a reason to have opened fire on me. He told me to be patient.

One night I smelt burning. Soon enough the word was passed down the wing that someone had set themselves alight. The prison seemed to physically shake and rock with the response, as if there had been an earthquake. I had never heard anything like it. I mean, there were more than 500 women in Holloway and they were all going nutty, jumping up and down. But it wasn't because there was a woman on fire. They knew the fire brigade had turned up and they were all screaming at the firemen out in the yard, 'Get 'em off, gorgeous,' and, 'Get over here and get your kit off, mate.' All that sort of stuff and they were jumping up and down like wild women.

The firemen lapped it up. They didn't exactly break any world records putting the fire out. It was more like they were on the catwalk – posing, waving and blowing kisses, flexing their muscles at us lot behind bars. I mean, there was a poor woman on fire and this lot thought they were film stars. You can imagine what would have happened if the women had got their hands on them. They would have been raped. Some of these women hadn't been with a man for years. I mean, firemen are a turn-on even when you aren't in prison so, for us who were banged up, you girls out there know how good they would have looked. And the burnt woman? We were told later that she was OK but she had to go to hospital and we never did know exactly how bad it was.

I had first been allowed a bath after being inside just

over a week. Taking the bandages off had actually done me a favour because the wounds were healing better that way. But my so-called bath was just three inches of water. I stood there looking at it in disbelief.

'Yous lot are taking the piss,' I said.

One of the heavy mob took out a rule book and quoted from it. 'Category-A prisoners are to bathe once every ten days and three inches of water is to be used.'

I wasn't amused. This wasn't a bath, it was a puddle and I refused to get in. Then one of the screws said they knew I wouldn't get in it and at last they turned the taps on and filled up the bath properly. They thought they were doing me a favour but I told them their jobs had gone to their heads. I said I thought that they must have been bullied at school and that they were very sad.

The very next morning the heavy mob was back to take me back to Basildon University hospital for a check-up and to have my stitches removed. Eight of them took me to the minibus and then what looked like half of the British police force and army combined escorted me to the hospital. Roads had been shut off. Armed police units flanked the minibus and the hospital was crawling with officers. I was chained to one of the red-and-blacks and around ten armed police surrounded us.

All these normal people were walking through the hospital and I couldn't stop laughing. 'I'm innocent, I'm innocent!' I shouted but they wouldn't even look at me as they must have thought I was a terrorist or a mad woman. The security made me look like public enemy No. 1. I knew I was not what I had been made out to be. I never tried to kill anyone. So I just kept my head held high as we walked to the doctor's room.

I had about 350 stitches removed and all the time they wouldn't take the cuffs or chains off me. But I didn't care. I'd had a bit of a laugh at the hospital. I'd had the army come out because of me and I amused the doctors and nurses with a bit of banter. I wasn't pleased that they wouldn't take the cuffs of but rules are rules, I suppose. All was well with my wounds, which was a big relief and lucky given the way I went without a bath in my unhygienic cell for over a week.

I learned that I had further charges to face. I had taken the blame for having the ammonia bottle, knuckle duster and joint in my van so that Matt wouldn't get done for them. Now that little incident reared its ugly head and, having been arrested for it in Kent, I was taken to Ashford magistrates court. I'd already said I was guilty but I still had to appear in court. Inevitably, out came the armed police escort and they even locked the court doors. I swear the three magistrates looked at me with pure terror in their eyes. Only God knew what the police had told them about me. But I was in cuffs and they had no need to worry. When my solicitor spoke, it quickly turned out that this relatively minor case was being dropped because the attempted-murder charge was so severe.

I just thought to myself that God had got a full-time job looking after me and I thanked him with all my heart and soul as I left the court that day. Of course, I was still worried about the attempted-murder charge but this was a result and a step in the right direction.

God smiled on me again because there was more good news after I'd been in Cat A for about two months. Gary Jacobs was convinced by then I hadn't fired a shot and was determined to build a good case in my defence. I grew to like Gary because I told him from my heart that I had not tried to kill anyone and he believed me and, on that basis of trust, he fought my corner.

He arrived as usual one day with a big smile on his face. 'It's great news, Jane,' he said before he had even sat down in the visiting room. 'The Home Office forensics report into the shooting shows your gun was not fired. It proves you did not try to kill anyone and that the police claims are wrong. There is no way you can now face attempted-murder charges against two officers. I'm delighted to tell you, Jane, that this means the police evidence against you on these major charges has crumbled.'

I was virtually speechless but managed to say, 'Thank you so much. I told you I was innocent.'

'Well, we still have a way to go on the other charges but it's a major step forward,' he said.

Poor Gary passed away in 2002 but I'd like to thank him and his partner Sunhil for their faith and hard work. They knew I was a villain but they believed in my innocence and had too much respect for the law just to take the easy path. They were good and honest men.

The night after that meeting with Gary I went back to my cell, believing my luck was finally changing for the better. I read the bible again and I found it a real comfort. Not as big a comfort as the fact of that police case against me crumbling though. That was Gary's word – 'crumbling' – and it kept going through my head as I read on. There were a lot of the names in the bible I couldn't pronounce properly but I liked and understood the stories.

The Governor turned up later on his nightly visit with more good news. 'You are no longer a Cat A prisoner, Lee,' he said. 'As from tomorrow your Cat A status will be removed and you will be relocated in the prison.'

This was brilliant news and there was a very good reason I was no longer Cat A. The forensics had proved my guns hadn't been fired at all on the night of the job, just as Gary had said, so I could no longer be treated as a dangerous woman. Things were now moving fast and in my favour. My excitement at being moved to a new cell after two months in Cat A soon turned to disappointment. The only difference in standard was that there was a small, square tin mirror on the wall, a table and chair made of wood instead of cardboard and I had a real bed with a real mattress instead of a concrete shelf. I don't know what I expected but it was a bit more than that.

But things were going my way, I told myself. I'd got

off on the squirter, knuckle duster and joint charges and now I wasn't going to face an attempted-murder charge. OK, things were not great but they had got a lot, lot better. And now the cops knew they were wrong to have shot at me, which was definitely in my favour, so I was looking on the bright side for the first time in ages. Gary told me to hang in there because I was still facing armed-robbery charges.

The Governor told me I was still top security so for the first few days in my new cell I wasn't allowed out. I was still what was known inside as 'behind the door' but I was now allowed regular baths and all the things that my family had sent me, including a hairdryer, clothes and pictures of my family. It was a lot better than Cat A because other inmates could come and talk to me through the door. I started to feel a lot better. Then other inmates told me about a bully on the wing who had been stealing. I made a mental note not to let that happen to me. I hadn't met this woman and I didn't like her already. She had been robbing 'canteen' from other prisoners. Canteen was really important in making life a little more bearable. On remand you could spend up to £100 a week on tobacco, chocolate, biscuits, tea bags, sugar, phone cards, make-up and toothpaste. Once convicted you could only spend about £25, which made life less pleasant. This was the general idea, I supposed. The way it worked was you got sent postal orders from the outside world and converted them to prison money. Matt was sending me money in every week without fail.

Almost a month after I had been taken off Cat A I was allowed out of my cell. This was the first time I had been allowed out without the heavy mob and the first time the prison didn't have to go on lockdown when I was out. So what did I do? I walked into the dining hall and shouted, 'Who's the fucking bullying cow I don't stop hearing about nicking off people and picking on them?'

The whole dining hall went quiet. Even the screws just stood there until, lo and behold, the mouthy cow jumped up and, before she could say a word, I was on top of her. I grabbed her and started punching her. I was beating the living daylights out of her and I swear the screws gave me a few seconds – which was all I needed – before they hit the alarm bell. They knew she was a wrong 'un and needed sorting and they let me do it for them.

In came the heavy mob with riot shields, helmets and batons and I was dragged back to my cell. You might imagine this did not go down too well with the Governor just a few days after my Cat A status had been revoked. I was taken before him the same day.

'Are you out of your mind?' he asked, genuinely confused but angry at the same time. 'You have been off Cat A for nearly a month and this was the first time you were allowed out of your cell and you went and beat the living daylights out of another inmate, who is now in the hospital wing. What have you got to say for yourself?'

'It wasn't me, Governor,' I said.

He wasn't happy with that answer. 'Don't take the

piss out of me, Lee,' he growled. 'Fifteen of my officers had to drag you off the girl. Now, what do you have to say for yourself?'

'Honest, sir, it wasn't me,' I repeated.

He gave up. 'Well, it's you who is going to have to spend one week in the block and then three weeks behind your cell door with all you privileges stopped,' he said. 'That's three weeks' loss of canteen privileges and thirty days on top of your eventual sentence. So tell me what you have to say for yourself, Lee.'

'Thank you, Guv,' I said.

'Get her out of my sight,' he snarled at the screws.

So I was in the block, which was solitary imprisonment. It was like Cat A all over again but I was OK because it was essentially all I knew of life in prison and I just kept reading the bible. When my dad next visited, he wasn't pleased. I told him not to worry and that I was OK. During the visit all the other inmates were coming up to me and telling me, 'Well done,' for getting the bully. They were introducing themselves and I swear that by the end of the visit my dad knew more of the inmates than I did. They all told him he had nothing to worry about and that I could look out for myself. Anyway, they said that they would look out for me as well after what I had done to the bully.

'I don't know, my girl,' Dad said before he left. 'What are we going to do with you? You're a one off, all right.' But he left with a smile on his face and that was all I was worried about.

I only did a week in the block before I was returned to my cell. Everyone was coming up to my door thanking me and praising me for doing the bully. It was a hero's reception, all right. I was still behind the door for three weeks with loss of canteen privileges but my new friends made sure I didn't go without. I ate like a queen, as the girls who worked in the kitchen gave me fruit and cakes. At one point I had five pillows and five blankets in my cell and you were only meant to have one of each. They brought me phone cards and tobacco, which I wasn't allowed because of the loss of my privileges. They all rallied around me and got me by. When they were allowed out of their cells, they took turns to come to my door and chat to me so I wasn't alone all the time. I couldn't believe how nice these people were to me. I don't know what I expected but I was so touched by the kindness they were showing.

The girl who burned herself with cigarettes also made it into the general population – or normal location, as they call it. They put her in with an 18-year-old who was only in for playing her stereo too loud at night. What a joke that sentence was. I mean, take the stereo away but don't put the poor girl inside for something like that. One night I could hear the poor stereo kid screaming because the nutter who burned herself had gone mental. Well, she already was mental but you know what I mean. She attacked the other girl and I swear the poor girl was screaming for her life but I couldn't do anything to help. Nobody could. I started screaming for the screws to help her, kicked my door and caused a right racket. Everyone started banging their doors and screaming for help. When the screws did arrive, they could see what was going on through the slit in the door but they weren't able to do anything because they were not allowed in the cell after dark. Only the heavy mob could go in and they needed the permission of the Governor. I could see them all looking at what was going on. They told the nutter to leave her cellmate alone but she didn't.

'Fucking do something!' I screamed through my door. 'Get the kid out of there and put her in with me.'

'We cant do that because you are too dangerous,' said one of the screws.

I couldn't believe what I was hearing. All the time the nutter was punching the kid and threatening her. 'I'll read her a bedtime story and rock the poor kid to sleep but, for God's sake, get her out of there. She'll kill her,' I pleaded. 'What that mad cow does to her will be on your heads.'

Eventually, the heavy mob got permission to get her out and put her in another cell for the night. But that kid tried to commit suicide three times after that night. And all she ever did was play her music too loud. She wasn't a villain and it just showed what prison can do to people. Word got around that the neighbour outside who had first complained about her music was a magistrate so we all knew why she got time for so-called antisocial behaviour. I don't know how these people can sleep at night.

I was fuming about the whole incident. As soon as I was allowed out of my cell after the three weeks were up, I got the nutter. I smashed her all over the place. I really wanted to kill her but the heavy mob dragged me off and I was back down the block and in front of the Governor again. 'I have just been informed by my security staff that you were acting in self-defence,' he said, to my astonishment.

I was going say it wasn't me, just like the last time, but instead I said, 'Yes, sir. It was self-defence.' So I didn't get punished for that one and I must say the heavy mob earned my respect that day. Don't get me wrong. I didn't tell them anything and they were not my friends when I was inside but they got my respect. When I was taken back to my cell, they said, 'Well done,' because they wanted to do the nutter too. I had done their job for them. It was funny how things worked out sometimes behind bars.

I had now been inside for three months and I'd heard no more about the charges against me. I was allowed out of my cell again to associate with the other inmates. I met a girl off my manor in Rainham. She was called Den and remembered the big yellow van I used for doing the beer run. She said she was there when I attacked the two Irish blokes – the two who were going to kidnap John – with my sword. We both had a laugh about that. It turned out that we were in neighbouring cells so one of us would hang a mirror out of the cell window and we could see each other while we chatted. We became best mates inside.

Den and I were eventually moved to a dormitory with a girl from Liverpool, a gypsy girl, an Indian girl and a Greek girl. Den was in for supplying Class A drugs, the scouser for fraud, the Indian girl for the murder of her lover, the Greek for importing cocaine and the gypsy girl for credit-card fraud. We were all on remand awaiting trial and we all had a great laugh together. All of us planned to plead not guilty and one night the Scouse girl suggested we try a Ouija board.

'I don't know about that,' I said. 'I'm fucking scared of anything like that.' But I agreed because I really did want to know what the future held.

So that night, when the lights went out, we played the board. I said to the Indian girl, 'Did you do the murder?' She said, 'No.' I asked the board and it said she did.

'You fucking liar,' I said. I couldn't stop laughing.

'Jane,' she said, 'I've got a couple of problems over his death.'

'Well, tell us what they are and we'll try to help you if we can,' I said.

'The police found his blood in the boot of my car.'

'Fucking hell, girl. That's a serious problem,' I said. 'What's the other one? We'll come back to that one, as that's a bit tricky.'

'They found his body buried in my back garden,' she said.

She was so right and proper it was hilarious. She looked like butter wouldn't melt but, to be fair, she looked bang to rights here and the board agreed.

'Fucking problems!' I said. 'They are more than fucking problems, girl. I can't help you. You need God's help. He's the only one who can help you now.'

I felt for this girl and I came to totally respect her. She was trapped in an arranged marriage and hated her husband because she still loved her childhood sweetheart. But the husband got jealous and killed him and then got her involved in hiding the body. How sad was that for her? The husband was also in jail for the murder but I thought the Indian girl was innocent. He was the real guilty party.

Anyway, we asked the board what the verdict would be at her trial and it said she would be found not guilty so she was over the moon. And believe me when I tell you that this board was for real. It was. I know it sounds soppy. But read and learn.

The board told Den she would get a five stretch and the Greek that she would get eleven years. Now, the Greek girl was innocent, as God is my witness, having been set up by a so-called friend who secretly put liquidised cocaine in bottles of rum she brought into the country. The board said I would get bail on 11 May 1998 and also said I wouldn't come back to prison. The scouser would get 18 months and the gypsy girl would be released the very next day.

'How?' asked the gypsy and the board said she

would get bail. 'I can't' she said. 'I haven't even gone for bail.'

Well, some of us got to hear what we wanted and some didn't but we all believed it was real, that night in prison. The ones who got bad news from it put it down to a bad spirit.

'And bad spirits lie,' said the gypsy girl.

The next day the gypsy wanted to do the board again because it said she would get out that very day. So we did it again she asked the board if she would get bail and again it said, 'Yes.' She asked when and it said at 2.45pm that same day. It was already 3.30pm so our confidence in the board was shaken, to say the least. But the gypsy totally believed the board and started ringing the bell for the screws to come. When they arrived, she said she wanted to talk to her solicitor on the phone straight away. The screws let her ring him and – you are not going to believe this – I swear, as God is my witness, her solicitor told her she shouldn't be in there. She had been granted bail at 2.45pm that day. So she told the screws and they checked the fax machine in the office and, sure enough, a fax had just arrived from the court informing the prison that she had been granted bail.

Well, this board game became our best mate. I asked it once if it minded us doing it and it said, 'No,' but when I asked if it was bad to do it, it said, 'Yes,' and we never did it again. But I'd just like to say that everything it said about our sentences came true. Den got five years, the Indian girl was found not guilty, the Greek girl, who was innocent, got eleven years and I got bail on 11 May 1998.

The Indian girl was spending her £100 a week in canteen but saw none of the goodies. I asked her what was going on. She told me a Colombian drug baron, who was doing 25 years and so wasn't eligible for as much canteen as those on remand, was giving her money and the goods were all going back to her.

'What do you get out of the deal?' I asked.

'Nothing,' she said.

'Tell the Colombian you are not doing it any longer,' I said.

'No way. I'm terrified of her, Jane,' my pal said and showed me a threatening letter from the drug baron. 'She's very powerful. This isn't your normal drug dealer. She is in here for a couple of tons of coke.'

Well, I wasn't amused. 'I'll sort it,' I said. 'I don't care who she is out there in the world because in here she is an inmate like you and me and I am not having her frightening me and mine.'

I took my mate to the bullying baron and told her she had taken the piss long enough and that now it was over. The baron looked at my mate and told her she would do as she was told or she knew what would happen. I could see I was not getting through to this bitch so I grabbed her by the throat and, when she opened her mouth, I stuck the threatening letter in it. 'You lay one finger on her or her family outside and I give you my word of honour you won't ever leave this

I'm Jane Lee – otherwise known as the Gran.

Inset: Me in the middle, flanked by my brother John on the left and Shell on the right.

Me and my Staffordshire bull terrier Buller.

My son John and me.

Above: Matt – my love.

Below: Sharon the gypsy queen – who was always there for me – with her husband Clint and me.

Above: My son going clay pigeon shooting at the age of 8.

Below: Me and John.

Above: Me and John.

Below: Barbecue with me and John to the right and his friend Kirk on the left.

Me.

prison alive,' I told her. 'Now apologise to her or I'll kill you now.'

The bully totally changed her tune and apologised. In fact, she started trying to kiss and cuddle her victim. My mate had a heart of gold, poor girl, and that is what bullies thrive on. Every Sunday my mate's religious leader from her community brought her homemade Indian food. From that day on she shared it with me and her new friends. And believe me, it was the best Indian food I have ever tasted.

My dad was still visiting me every day without fail and John came with him sometimes. John was making me so proud and he never complained. He was doing really well. He was always with Shell's boys Darren, Kevin and Dean. I missed him so much but a big part of me didn't want him to see me in that situation. He was only 12 and prison wasn't the place for kids. I talked to him on the phone every day anyway.

Then came the day when Dad was late and I immediately got worried because his visits ticked by like clockwork. He had been a rock for me. I waited until the end of visiting time and he still hadn't shown up so I rang home and got my mum. I could hardly believe my ears. 'Your dad has been in tears here, girl,' Mum said. 'He turned up as normal but was told you had refused his visit. What were you playing at?'

'I wouldn't do that, Mum,' I told her. 'The screws told me he didn't turn up.'

Then the penny dropped. A nasty screw had told Dad

I didn't want to see him that day and told me he hadn't turned up. A despicable, outright lie. I'd been done. And what this screw had done was well below the belt. If she had a problem with me, she should have come to me and not used my dad. The moment I found out, I just lost the plot. I let the phone drop, ran into the screws' office and dived on the first officer I could find and started punching her. Of course, the heavy mob were called and they gave me a pasting but I got a few of them first. They weren't even the ones who had lied to my dad but at that moment they were all the same to me – scum.

I was back down the block for a week again and I swear, if I'd got hold of the screw who upset my dad, I would have killed her but I never did get to know who it was. The next time Dad came I apologised to him for what had happened, even though it wasn't my fault. But he didn't look right and, when I asked him what the matter was, he said he thought he might have had a stroke the night before. And I could see his face looked different – a little bit one-sided. I couldn't believe he had come to see me and not gone to the hospital first.

'Get to the hospital now, Dad,' I said. 'Just go.'

'But I couldn't miss your visit, girl,' he said.

I packed him off straight away. I had never before cried when I was in prison. Police, bullets, Cat A and wars with villains on the outside had never made me cry either but that day the tears were running down my face. My dad was right. He'd had a stroke and was in hospital for three weeks but he had battled to Holloway from the East End to be there for me. I thought that said everything I needed to know about my dad. Tough, loyal and full of love for me and his family. I love you so much, Dad.

My latest brush with the heavy mob led to me being moved into another dorm after I'd done my time in the block. The first minute I was in there I realised it was a Yardie dorm. There were four Jamaican gangsters in there – and me. They were proper Yardies, from Kingston, Jamaica. They were not amused that a whitey had been put in with them. And I can't blame them, to be honest, because they are very private people and, as far as they were concerned, I was invading their space. But there was nothing I could do about it when the screws were clearly having a good laugh at my expense. They put me there deliberately.

I could see the Yardies had got the hump but I still politely said, 'Hello.' They blanked me so I went straight to my bunk. Then their leader, Big Momma, sucked her teeth at me and I thought, 'Here we go.' As I was unpacking, they talked to themselves in patois – Yardie language – so that I couldn't understand them. In the end, nothing happened right then but there was a frosty atmosphere for a few days until I dropped something on the floor. It made a bit of noise and it was the opportunity Big Momma had been waiting for.

'Why you make dat noise and ting, bitch?' she said and started sucking her teeth. Well, my attitude was that it was fine not to talk but I wasn't going to let them bully me. It was time for them to meet the Gran. I jumped up and walked over.

'I'll fucking kill the lot of yous,' I said, looking straight at Big Momma. 'Let's fucking have it. If today's the day I die, it's a good day to die.'

That rocked her. To my amazement, she did something totally unexpected. 'Me sorry, sister. Me don't mean nuttin',' she said.

I told her I hadn't done her any harm and didn't want to and from then on we all became good friends. In fact, I really got to like them. And they started teaching me a few Yardie phrases. Even so, I used to tie a pen in my hair for protection, which was just as well because I needed it when I had a run-in with the very top Yardie. She was another Big Momma – I'll call her Big Momma 2, to avoid confusion.

Big Momma and Big Momma 2 were co-defendants charged with smuggling coke. Now Big Momma 2 was not big at all. She was tiny but they called her Big Momma because she was the very top Yardie. She wasn't happy that I'd offered her mate out and it was something she had to be seen to be doing something about. She had a reputation to keep.

Big Momma 2's crew did everything for her, fetching and carrying all the time. The only thing they couldn't do was get her food for her at meal times because it was prison rules that everyone had to get their own. So what she used to do was push in the queue and everyone would let her do it, even though she was small. Nobody wanted to deal with the rest of them. It didn't bother me until the day she brushed me aside when I was right at the front. She just gave me this cold look as if to say, 'Out of the way, Whitey.' Well, as you will know well by now, I wouldn't have that. Not at all. I grabbed the plate off the kitchen worker who was dishing up the food and smashed it over Big Momma 2's head. Then I grabbed her around the neck and pulled the pen from my hair and held it to her neck, gouging it in so she knew I wasn't messing about. Big Momma 1 just stood back because she knew me well enough by now to know I would use the pen.

'Stay the fuck back,' I said to all the Yardie crew, 'or she's getting it in the neck. It's a fucking good day to die,' I whispered in the ear of Big Momma 2. 'But if I go, you are coming with me.'

Someone shouted out from the crowd, 'You're a dead woman.' But I ignored that and gave my attention entirely to Big Momma 2.

'I'm game if you are, babe. You started this by pushing in and I am not having that,' I said. 'I am no better nor any worse than you so I'm not standing for it. I'll die defending my self-respect because it means a lot to me. The ball's in your court.'

While this was going on, the inmates were blocking off the screws who were trying to get to us. Then Big Momma 2 spoke for the first time. 'Leave the armed robber alone, girls,' she ordered her crew. 'We haven't got no problem. The armed robber, she's OK.'

I gradually relaxed my grip on her to see if she was going to keep her word.

'They have been telling me about you, girl,' she said. She didn't look rattled at all. She was as calm as you like for someone who nearly had a pen through their jugular. 'You got some balls on you. Glad to make your acquaintance.'

'You aren't lacking in that department yourself, are you?' I said.

'Respect,' she said.

The screws were asking everyone what all the kerfuffle was about but everything was sweet. In fact, putting me in with the Yardies had backfired big time on the screws because now we were all pals. So what did the screws do? Moved me out of the Yardies' dorm and back in with my old pals.

I was losing track of time but I must have been in for about four or five months by then and my case was starting to look good. I still had serious charges hanging over me but it was beginning to look like the police knew they shouldn't have shot me. Gary told me I was almost certain to get bail, as the cops knew their evidence wouldn't stand up in court against the rock-solid forensic report, so he told me we were going to go for bail on 11 May – just as the Ouija board had said.

Finding £10,000 bail wasn't a problem but getting someone to stand up for me who was of good character and didn't have convictions was slightly trickier. A rich mate whose family ran a haulage firm got her mum to speak for me when I appeared at Snaresbrook crown court. I'd never met the mum before and, when I got to court, I didn't connect her with a woman I saw who was not sitting with my family. This woman was on her own, suited and booted and, to be honest, I thought she was someone from the court. She kept waving and smiling at me and I thought she was trying to make me look dodgy so I gave her a dirty look and that soon made her stop. Then one of the court officials asked who was putting up bail and she stood up. She told the court she was my aunt and that I had lived with her for most of my youth and that she was willing to put up bail. I felt like a right fool. I wished someone had told me what was going on. I had to agree to stay at her house and I was then returned to Holloway to wait for the bail money to be transferred.

My dad was waiting for me later that day with my rich mate and we went home, where John was waiting. We all cried buckets. But they were tears of happiness. I was so proud of John. It didn't matter what had happened, he never complained. He was just so happy that we were back together as a family. As for me, I had been locked up for six months and I felt so happy to be out. I had to be at home with John and I broke my bail conditions straight away by not staying at the house of the lady who appeared in court on my behalf. I wanted to get back to normal life and felt it was only a small risk to take.

I was at home a couple of weeks when I saw the

middle-man who had passed on the dodgy speed from those so-called gangsters all those months earlier. He invited me to a party. John was staying with a mate so I agreed. But it all went wrong when some blokes at the party started fighting. All of a sudden it was the last place I wanted to be while out on bail. People were going nutty and someone got stabbed and I knew had to get out of there. The law was on its way. I could even hear the sirens as I legged it down the stairs. I walked out of the front door and there were police everywhere. I calmed down, took a deep breath and walked off, minding my own business. I got stopped by an officer. 'Have you just left that party?' he asked.

'What party, officer?' I replied. 'I'm just on my way to work.'

He told me to be on my way and, even though I didn't have a clue where I was, I just kept walking until I came to a train station. It was 4.30am. I went to sleep on a bench and waited for the 6am train. It was 8am before I got home. I'd had a narrow escape. If they had caught me in breach of my bail conditions, I would have back inside immediately. What an idiot I had been but I had also been lucky – again.

I liked to think I had learned my lesson. I knew my trial was coming up and I kept out of trouble. I couldn't let my boy and my dad down again. I wouldn't be telling the truth if I didn't say I was worried. Don't get me wrong. I knew I could do the time but this was all about John. I had to be there for him and knew that more than ever now. My trial was at Snaresbrook crown court, where Gary told me the police wanted to do a deal because they were worried about any comeback over my shooting. An investigation by the Police Complaints Commission had taken place into the incident, he said, and the police were not looking as if they came out of it too well. It looked as if the officer had panicked when he opened fire because I had not fired a shot and there was no evidence to show I had been trying to run anyone over either. Also, the fact that all the bullets had hit me from behind didn't look good for them. They couldn't even do me for the guns, as they were legal and Gary had already proved the black powder in the bullets was legal firework powder. It was a clause in the law. It all added up to one thing. The police wanted to do a deal.

'They want you to plead guilty to attempted robbery and dangerous driving and to possession of a Class B drug – that's the speed – in exchange for them dropping the attempted murder charges,' Gary explained. 'If you agree, you will walk out of this court a free woman. The judge will take into consideration the time you have done on remand and the fact that you were shot four times as punishment enough. But if you don't take the deal, they have told me the original attempted murder charges will stand and, if you are found guilty, you will be looking at double figures and could serve at least ten years in prison.'

I asked Gary what he thought and he told me it was

up to me. I knew I should get a 'not guilty' because the cops had told too many lies but, at the end of the day, it was up to the jury and, if I got a jury who were all for the police, I would be fucked.

I thought about it. I thought about the Greek girl who was innocent and got 11 years. I didn't try to kill the police and they knew it but I did do the robbery. If I won a trial, I would end up a rich woman because I would be free to go for compensation for being shot. But if I didn't, I would be leaving John out in the world all alone for a very long time. It didn't take more thinking. No amount of money was worth the risk of leaving my son. I took the deal.

The judge took into consideration my wounds and I got a two-year sentence, suspended for two years, and a three-year driving ban. I walked out of that court a free woman with my head held high. My guns were confiscated and put in the police museum. That gave me the hump. The police asked the judge if the attempted-murder and firearms charges could be left on file and he agreed. I didn't take much notice of that, not realising that it meant I was on the police computer as having tried to murder two officers. Every time they looked me up, even if it was just for a parking ticket, I would come up as armed and dangerous and public enemy No 1. All I cared about that day was walking free. And walk free I did.

When I got home, I was told I had to go to Ilford police station to collect all the legitimate guns and rifles the police had taken from my home in black bags the night I was shot. In all, they had about five bags of my belongings. A friend went with me and, when we got there, we were taken into a room, where my stuff was and the officer in charge had five sheets of paper with everything listed on it. He started going through the bags one by one and had ticked off about five of the items after searching through the bags when he said, 'Jane, it's all here but it's going to take all day to go through this lot. Just sign here and you can take the lot.'

'OK,' I said and signed. I couldn't wait to get out of there.

'I hope yous ain't going to shoot me again,' I joked with him.

'Don't worry, Jane, no one's going to shoot you,' he said and we left for home. We went through the bags and found the Billy was still with the rest of my belongings, nicely sealed in two forensic-evidence bags. Rather than destroying it, they had mistakenly left it with the rest of my belongings. Me and my mate couldn't believe it.

'What idiots,' I said. We couldn't stop laughing.

It was only a small amount of Billy – a couple of ounces – but I was back in business. You must think I was mad going straight back into crime but all my money was gone now because I had been inside for six months. I had to survive and, anyway, I said to my mate, if I ever got nicked for selling Billy and they asked me who supplied me, I could tell them it was the police. And I had the forensic bags to prove it.

There were people saying that, after what I'd been through, I would never pick up a gun again. How wrong they were. The low-life scum who had set me up to be shot were now my top priority.

10

FREEDOM

*I was still ducking and diving for a living
but it wasn't easy.*

I had been out a few months and things were returning
to normal. Well, normal in my world. Matt was over
the moon. We still weren't together but I still loved him
with all my heart. The lover I once knew had now
become my soul mate. It was a bond which would last a
lifetime and I was prepared to die for him.

He had been there for me through it all. He had even
taken a bullet because of me. He never said why he got
shot when I was in hospital but I knew it must have been
because he had gone after the grasses that were
responsible for me ending up in prison. All he had told
me about it was that he had come out of a house and
somebody had been hiding in the bushes and shot him.
Matt never saw their faces but he was certain it was the

grasses and now they were living in fear and had gone into hiding.

I knew we would get them, one by one, and took satisfaction from knowing that they were living in fear and that it was worse for them than it was for me. I was now free and it had all backfired on them. I once believed there was honour among thieves. How naïve I was. I had found out the hard way and now I found it hard to trust anyone except my family and Matt. But those grasses knew we would be coming. I enjoyed my life being back at home but we both wanted them sorted. Now our wounds had healed, it was time for payback. We went out to war and got them back one by one.

The bloke who gave me the information about the robbery in the first place had his businesses destroyed. And then I read in the news that the two boys who were supposed to have come with me on the job had been kneecapped. No one was ever charged. I don't know anything more than that about those cases but, let's be honest, that's exactly what they deserved. An eye for an eye, in my book. A couple of others from their crew got away but that's snides and grasses for you – they have to be good runners!

Life went on. I was indoors one night with my son and my two Alsatians, Will and Max. The dogs were a big part of my family. I loved them both like they were babies. This particular night Will was in the garden and wouldn't come inside. Now, these dogs slept in my bed, they sat on my leather settees and only went out to the garden to go the toilet. But Will wouldn't come in. It was 2.30am and I wanted to go to bed. So I left Will out there and Max and I went to bed. I had been in bed for about half an hour when I heard Will barking and growling, and I knew someone was out there. Whenever I heard my dogs bark, I knew there was someone walking past or coming down the path. But when they growled, it meant danger. Will knew long before me that someone was sneaking around and plotting me up. That's why he wouldn't come in. I grabbed my M16 rifle and ran straight downstairs but I was too late. I had a side gate and the intruder had jumped over it, though not before Will bit them. I ran back through the house just in time to see the snoopers jump into a van. There were three of them, all men. I aimed my rifle and shot at them but they were already taking off.

My neighbour heard the noise and came running out of her house just as I fired. She asked me if I wanted her to call the police. She had startled me and, instinctively, I spun around, forgetting I still had the rifle in my hands. I pointed it straight at her and said, 'Don't you dare.' She looked terrified and I suddenly realised what I had done. 'I'm so sorry, babe. I didn't mean to point the gun at you,' I said.

She knew I didn't mean any harm and replied, 'Oh, Jane, you're so brave. What would happen if they had burgled me? There is no way I could stand up for myself the way you do.'

I told her the burglars were scum and would stab anyone in their sleep. I hated burglars and I was bang in the mood for a battle with them. The Gran had come out and I was on one. I put a chair on the doorstep and sat there with my rifle in my lap all night waiting, just in case they came back. But nobody came. In the morning the milkman arrived and, when he saw me my gun, he said, 'Fucking hell! Who are you expecting? Jessie James and his gang? It's like the bleedin' Wild West. I deserve danger money coming here.' He was OK, my milkman. I used to sell him beer and fags when I was doing the beer run.

'Three men tried to burgle me last night.'

'They must have a death wish or something,' he said as he carried on with his milk round.

I went back inside, as I was looking a bit of a nutter, all tooled up out on my doorstep in broad daylight. But I stayed awake for three nights running waiting for them to come back. People work all their lives for what they have got and the likes of these scummy burglars wanted to take it away from them. Some things have value beyond money in a family home and can never be replaced. These scum would sell anything for a quick fix of crack. Well, I hated them. Go and rob a bank or go and nick from a shop if you need money but don't go into ordinary homes.

By the end of my vigil I was so tired that I couldn't keep my eyes open, though I wouldn't take my eyes off the front path for a moment. I was in warrior mode and fully armed. I was so armed up I could have taken on a small army if it came down my path. Let's be honest here, it might not have been burglars. It could have been the enemy, as I had done a few scum in my time who might want payback. Bring it on, I thought to myself. I was ready and waiting. If they had come back, I would have given them a war and they would never have left alive.

I was so hungry and a little woozy from the sleep deprivation so I put a treacle pudding on the gas – the kind you boil in the tin. I went back to my lookout duties and was waiting for it to finish cooking when all of a sudden I heard an almighty bang in the kitchen. I thought I'd been bombed but, when I dashed into the room, all I could see was treacle pudding dripping off everything. It was all over the ceiling, all over the sink and the cooker too. Everything was covered in treacle. I must have dropped off to sleep and it had boiled dry and then exploded. I was too shattered to clean it up so I just threw the pot in the sink and went to bed. I knew by now the intruders were not coming back. They hadn't got the balls. This kind of scum only crept around when they thought you were asleep or they stabbed you in the back. They probably thought I had lost my touch when I was shot and now fancied their chances. Well, when I shot at them as they ran away, they found out my touch had just got a whole lot touchier.

When I woke up, I made a point of apologising again to my neighbour for frightening her with my rifle. I told her I was always there for her and her family if ever they needed me. She told me that she knew I hadn't meant to frighten her and that she was OK. 'You are a bit nutty, Jane, but I like you, girl,' she said and we had a good laugh about the treacle pudding too.

By now Mum wasn't very well. In fact, she'd had cervical cancer for several years and, despite the treatment, she was just getting worse. She was also suffering with breathing problems and Dad had his hands full looking after her. Mum had started to suffer with the disease well before I was shot but, nevertheless, she had often looked after John and the dogs when I was inside. We'd had our differences in the past but that time she did me proud. Now she was in a bad way and I was being extra careful to stay out of trouble for her sake. My family just couldn't have handled any more problems but I still needed to make money. I didn't have qualifications, I hadn't long been out of prison and hopes of somebody employing me were slim. So I had to support John the only way I knew how. I was still ducking and diving for a living but it wasn't easy. Don't get me wrong. I wasn't getting rich and I wasn't robbing people's homes or causing misery with hard drugs like crack and heroin. That was not my game. Yet I knew I was doing wrong and by now I wished I could find another way.

One day I was going to pick up a bit of Billy and on the way back my worst fears came true. Two police cars pulled me over and I gave the questioning officer a dodgy name because I knew they had my card marked.

'Really,' he said. Where is Jane then?' It was all innocent-like but they knew. They searched me, found the speed and I was arrested. I also had a joint's worth of puff in my pocket and, in the end, I would be charged with possession of puff, possession of Billy and driving while on a three-year ban. I immediately thought I'd been set up again. The car I was in was not in my name so how did they know it was me? At least when they asked where I got the Billy from, I was ready. I said, 'The police gave it to me. Honest.' They were not amused. They must have thought they had heard it all but this time it was actually the truth.

I just didn't have the heart to tell the family I'd been nicked again. They had been through enough but, as I came close to my court date, returning to Snaresbrook to have my case heard, I knew I was going down. What a mess I'd made of everything. Then came a real bombshell. My mum died of cancer. She was just 54. It was a sad, sad time. I realised how her hard life had taken its toll on her, especially in her early years as an 18-year-old mum with three kids and three jobs. But Mum and I had got closer again and, although I had spent much of my life not getting on with her, we had made our peace towards the end. She had been there for me when I was away. She wrote to me every day.

At court the charge relating to the speed was dropped

as I produced the forensic bags to my solicitor and explained what had happened. They had denied giving the speed to me. But how had I got the forensic bags then? True, it wasn't the same speed that they had given me but they couldn't prove that. So the case was adjourned for a couple of weeks for it all to get sorted out. I was bailed to reappear and was allowed to go home. To be honest though, I didn't have a good feeling. Even though the charges were not that serious, I was still on a two-year suspended sentence, which could be enforced if I did anything wrong during that two years. I cursed myself, as I realised this little bit of bother could have big consequences.

I thought I was definitely going to do time but I still couldn't bear to tell Dad because he had so much on his plate with Mum's death. He didn't need me giving him more grief than he already had. I just wanted to forget about everything but it was weighing on my mind. My John was only 15 and that was my main worry. He had grown up fast and I knew he could look after himself but he was still a boy and I was feeling so guilty. Even though I hadn't been sent down yet, I cheered him up by buying him a Porsche and a Rolex watch. He had already learned to drive at a nearby driving centre equipped with traffic lights and roundabouts. He paid a couple of quid and could stay there as long as he like. John loved it, became a good driver and was over the moon with the Porsche. I had already bought him an Escort XR2 and found the white Porsche 944 in the local paper. It was beautiful. The roof could be taken off, it had leather seats and it was my way of getting him ready for what I knew was coming. Unfortunately, things went a little bit wrong.

I told him he wasn't allowed to drive on the roads because he would get pulled. But did he listen to me? No. But I couldn't blame him. He was 15 and behind the wheel of a Porsche. I blamed myself for the inevitable. He was out, loving it, when I got a phone call from the police.

'We've arrested your son. Can you come to Romford police station, please, Miss Lee?' the officer said.

I phoned Tracey and we both went to hear the story. John had been chased and arrested trying to get away. It wasn't too hard for the police to spot him in a white Porsche but, before they could get near him, he pulled over, threw the keys out of the car and legged it with his mate who had been in the passenger seat.

When I arrived at the police station, I was taken into an interview room and questioned about the car. 'Where did a 15-year-old boy get a Porsche from?' one of the officers asked.

'His dad bought it for him,' I said. 'I bought him a new pair of trainers so his dad had to go one better and buy him a Porsche.'

'Where did he learn to drive like that? It took my best drivers to catch him,' the officer said.

'His dad taught him.'

'And where does his dad live?'

'Somewhere in Kent,' I said.

'Where in Kent?' he asked.

'I don't know, officer. I take full responsibility though because John shouldn't have been driving it unless he was in the Cardrome and I should have stayed with him.'

So they gave John a caution and impounded the car at a car pound at Upminster police station. They said they wanted to check out the paperwork on it and said I could pick it up in a couple of days. Well, a week went by and I hadn't heard from them. So I phoned up the police station and they said I could pick it up on Monday but I was in court on Tuesday and I wasn't going to wait. I didn't have time. I knew I was going away and, if I didn't get this car now, I was not going to get it back so me and a mate went to get it from the pound.

The police station was closed so we went around the back to their pound. Luckily, the gates were open and the Porsche was sitting in sight. We didn't have the keys because John had thrown them out of the car when he was arrested so I phoned the AA. I was now in the police car pound with the AA man and my mate when a police officer came out the back door of the station to see what was going on.

'It's OK, officer,' I said. 'It's all been authorised.' The officer duly got in his car and left us to it. My friend couldn't believe it.

'You've got some bottle, girl,' she said under her breath

as the AA man – who also didn't know what was really going on – took the numbers from the barrel of the key locks and went to get me a key cut.

'Look,' I said to my friend, 'if I don't get this car today, I might not be able to get it back again, so needs must, girl.' Between me and the AA man, we got the car on the road. I treated him to a nice few quid for helping me.

On that Saturday night I got in John's Porsche and went for the freedom ride of my life, knowing in my heart that on Tuesday night I would back behind bars. I got myself all done up, filled the tank and went out and just drove. I drove all night. I raced anyone who was game. I mean, I was in a Porsche and, in my eyes, only a Ferrari could beat me and I won every race I got into. That drive made me happy and took my mind off my troubles. I felt as free as a bird.

On Sunday I packed all my prison stuff for court. I made sure everything was safe at home and that John understood the situation. That was the hardest part for me. But he was acting like a man by then and that helped a lot. I still hadn't told my family what was going on. I just didn't have the heart. I'd been so busy making sure everything was sorted for John. At last I went over to Shell's and asked her to come out with me and back at my place I broke the news that I was due in court the next day.

'I'm going down, Shell. I've been lucky so far but this time I can sense my luck has run out.' I told her all the details and she said I wouldn't go down but I knew the suspended sentence was not going away. 'I hope you're right, Shell,' I said, smiling, but I knew she was wrong.

The next morning I was all packed and ready to go. I had plugged a bar of puff up my crutch. That may not sound nice but it would make life a lot mellower inside. If I was going down, I was going down in style and I drove to Snaresbrook crown court in the Porsche with Shell and Tracey. When we got there, my barrister said I was looking at a community-service sentence, getting my hopes up a little bit. But that was the end of the good news. As soon as we were in the court room, the police handed the judge a note. While he was reading it, he didn't look too impressed. He kept glancing from the sheet of paper in his hand to me. My barrister started to talk but the judge just told him to be quiet. He turned to me and said he knew my barrister was going to try to convince him not to give me a custodial sentence but that it was not going to work. I glanced up at Shell and Tracey in the public gallery and winked at them. I knew I was going down and needed to be strong.

The judge continued. He said I was a very dangerous woman. He then said he was sentencing me to six months for driving on a ban and three months for possession of a Class B drug – that was the puff. Then he threw the book at me – I had one month left to go of that suspended sentence but he could invoke the whole two years. And he did. In all, I would serve two years and nine months, all to run consecutively. I was banned from driving for another three years and would have to retake my test. He had given me the maximum punishment he could. I looked at my sister again, waved her and Tracey goodbye and then I was led to the cells under the court to await the van to take me back to Holloway to start my sentence.

I must be honest, I was shocked – not that I let it show. But two years and nine months. I thought I'd get about a year. It was April 2000 and I'd had a year and 11 months of freedom. But now I had got a longer stretch than I had received when I was first sentenced.

11

BACK INSIDE – HER MAJESTY'S PRISONS EAST SUTTON PARK AND COOKHAM WOOD

*Anyone who thinks he can harm my boy is
going to get buried today.*

When I got to Holloway, I knew nearly everyone. I'd got the nine-ounce bar of puff, which was to come in very handy. I had hidden it in the only place where the screws couldn't or wouldn't search. I must say, it was a lot easier knowing that I was going down, as I'd sorted everything out first. This time it didn't feel like I'd been dragged off the street and landed in prison unprepared.

I had to laugh because all I'd talked about in prison was when I was going to get out and what I was going to do. Prisoners all talked about how they were going to get a man and what they were going to do to him. And me being me, I was telling the girls before I left

Holloway last time that I was going to have non-stop sex. As it turned out, I had been out for nearly two years and didn't even kiss a man. Matt and I weren't together like that and I didn't want to be with anyone else. Not that my prison mates knew that and the first thing they wanted to know was all about my sex life. I lied. I told them that I hadn't stopped having sex since the last time I saw them. 'Oh, yes,' I said. 'We couldn't get enough of each other – morning, noon and night. We were doing it in the kitchen, the bedroom, the bathroom.' After all, it was what they wanted to hear and I think it cheered them all up.

The day after my arrival I was moved to East Sutton Park prison near Maidstone in Kent. By now Shell had told Dad what had happened and, when I phoned him, he was gutted. 'Why didn't you tell me, Jane?' he said. 'I could have stood up and spoke to the judge for you.'

'Dad,' I said, 'the judge wouldn't even let my barrister talk for me. The police gave him a letter and nothing could have saved me because of my suspended sentence. I'm sorry, Dad. I know you've been through enough with Mum dying and that's why I didn't want to worry you any more. You've been through enough with me too.'

John was staying at home this time, rather than with Dad. He had got plenty of money from me and he had his mates there for him. I knew it wasn't good but there was nothing else I could do. He was so grown up then. He had to grow up fast, just like I did. Anyway, my family was a phone call away if he needed anything and Shell and Matt were looking out for him.

It wasn't all bad. I couldn't believe my luck landing in East Sutton Park. This was an open prison and what a touch it was. It was like a big mansion house and it didn't even look like a prison. My best mate Den from Holloway had turned up as well, finishing off her five stretch. She had one month left. Her boy and mine were good mates and I was over the moon to see her. I even had the bed next to hers in the dorm and I soon settled in.

East Sutton Park was a lot more comfortable than Holloway but, if you did anything wrong, you could be sure the other inmates would grass you to the screws. Den told me the score. She warned me to keep myself to myself and not to trust anyone if I wanted to stay out of trouble and keep my place in the open prison. I didn't like those rules and yet I tried to keep them. But it didn't take long before I started getting the hump with the other inmates. 'Stool pigeons,' I called them. I swear to God, if you did something wrong, there wouldn't just be one but a queue of inmates at the office grassing you up. I couldn't handle it. I told Den I was going to explode.

'Please don't, Jane,' pleaded Den. 'I've only got three weeks left. Just keep your head down and keep yourself to yourself and you'll be OK. Please try and stay here until I go home.' I said I would do my best because I loved Den. She was on my level and it was good having her with me. I told her that, if anybody fucked with me, I'd do them after she left.

I got a job in the prison gardens trimming hedges. I was the strimmer girl and it was good. I could go anywhere in the grounds on my own with my strimmer. I could even go outside the prison and cut the hedges. What a difference it was to Holloway and a world away from Cat A. The only letdown was the other prisoners. Most of them seemed to think they were officers without keys. They weren't the hardened villains you got in Holloway and they would do anything to please the screws. And that was where we were different. When I went into the mansion house with my work boots on, another inmate once told me to take them off.

'You're not allowed to wear your work boots in the house,' she shouted and she was with a screw at the time.

I couldn't believe it and just lost it. 'Shut your fucking mouth. If you want my boots off that badly, you'll be taking 'em off with your fucking teeth.'

She was scared stiff and ran off and I got pulled into the office. I got a warning for that and a telling-off. Well, I could handle the officers pulling me up but not the inmates. No way. I told Den that I didn't think I'd last another three weeks. I had the bar of puff on me and I couldn't even have a joint with anyone in case they grassed me up. I'd go on the hill inside the grounds, outside the main building, and make myself a small joint, hoping no one would see me or report me to the officers.

When Den at last left, I was so happy for her, yet so sad that my friend had gone. I was sure I wasn't going to find any other friends like her. Then I met Sharon, a gypsy girl like me, and we were immediately friends. Sharon was inside for GBH on another bird but she was pukka and we got on like a house on fire. But, sadly for me, she was shipped straight out to another prison when her mum was caught chucking bottles of vodka over the fence to her. When I say caught, I mean another inmate grassed on her. But Sharon and I were kindred spirits and our paths would cross again.

Three days after Den left, a new shipment of prisoners arrived, including a French bird. She asked me what I was in for and how long I'd got. I told her I'd got two years and nine months for driving on a ban and having a bit of puff and she just laughed. I asked her what she was in for and she said she'd had a right touch. 'I'm in for importing a kilo of crack cocaine and a kilo of heroin and I only got eighteen months in an open prison.' Well, I lost it. She was laughing at me but I didn't find it funny. She was bringing heroin and crack into our country to kill our kids and only got 18 fucking months. I battered her. The screws came in force and dragged me off her, and that was the end of my time in East Sutton Park. I had told Den I'd only last three weeks after she went but I didn't last three days. But by that point I was past caring.

The next day I was moved out to Cookham Wood prison, near Rochester in Kent. There were loads of people I knew at Cookham Wood. I was well happy, daft as that sounds, because it was more like Holloway and not full of grasses. I phoned home and let Dad and John know I'd been moved but that everything was OK. Dad told me he was visiting John regularly, as he was the priority now, and that my boy was keeping my house spotless. I was really proud of him. Matt was looking out for John as well. In fact, everyone was but from a distance. He was 15 and was running our home like a proper man. With the money I'd left he was paying the rent to the council, as well as the bills, and Matt was going over every week to help out. The dogs were both fine and John was happy. I phoned him every day and he made me the proudest mum in this world. That boy deserved a knighthood the way behaved while I was away. He was on his own, with no brothers or sisters, and he was living in Essex and my family was in the East End. Matt was Kent, yet John was surviving in this mad world and doing it as best he could.

At Cookham Wood I told my mates I'd got a bar of puff when I was put on a wing with them. I was in a cell with one other inmate in what was called a two-up. But another mate assured me that the bird was safe so I was happy to go in with her. On the first night I asked the bird if she fancied a bit of puff.

'What? Drugs?' she replied. 'Oh no, I'll have none of that.'

So that night I laid on the top bunk and after lights out I rolled myself a big joint and got stoned. I was so stoned I couldn't keep my eyes open. The room was just one big bubble of smoke and I was smiling from ear to ear when I heard the bird ask, 'Is that puff I can smell?'

'No,' I told her.

But she jumped out of bed and I thought she was going for the buzzer to call the screws. Even though I was out of it and could hardly move, I was thinking I was going to have to do her. So I looked at her through the cloud of puff smoke and said, 'Listen, love, you can't smell anything, do you fucking understand me?'

She was looking at me and she realised that, if she touched that buzzer, she was in big trouble so she just said, 'OK. It's my mistake,' and got back into bed, much to my relief, as I didn't want to hurt this woman.

In the morning my mates were hysterical with laughter when I told them about it. They said they knew she didn't like puff but, as it was the only cell available in their wing, they told me she was safe. 'We knew you would sort her out anyway,' one of them said.

I wasn't amused. 'If I'd had to do her, I would have done you as well for putting me in that position.' We all burst into laughter.

I needed a single cell but you had to have 'enhanced' status to qualify and that meant you needed to be a goody two-shoes. Well, I am no goody and I can tell you now I was never in enhanced in the year I served in Cookham Wood. But I did need a single so I could puff in peace. I was selling some of my puff too but my roommate wasn't in on it and she didn't like the smoke after lights out so it was a problem. But then I was called to the office along with my mates. I was thinking I was in trouble when I was called in but my mates were told to wait outside. There was a screw who had noticed I'd been having all my gym clothes sent in by the Peacock Gym in the East End. She asked me how I knew the Peacock. I told her the owners were lifelong friends of mine. It turned out that she also knew the Peacock. In fact, he was another lifelong friend. What a touch. I thought I was going to be in trouble and this was the best result ever.

I opened the office door, called in my mates and told them that I knew the screw's family on the outside and that she was one of us. And she did become a loyal and good friend to me and my mates. She got us out of all sorts of trouble and told us which screws were safe. We had it good, thanks to her. I asked her if she could get me a single cell and she told me to go and see the doctor as he was the only one who could swing it. She said, 'You've only been in a couple of weeks and you've got to be in here at least six months to get enhanced status. If you get enhanced so soon, it's going to look dodgy.' Each of my mates who had been there over six months all got enhanced that week and our wing became the bollocks

I went to see the doctor about getting a single. I told him they had put me in a double with another inmate and it wasn't fair on her because I had nightmares. I told him I would jump around the room because I had bad dreams about being shot and at night I would think she was the policeman who shot me. I said, 'I really like her, doc, but she's terrified of me.' I was moved to a single cell that day for the other girl's safety. Another inmate who had been properly enhanced was moved back into a double because of me and that didn't go down too well with her. I told her you can be just a bit too good sometimes and laughed.

So I had the bar of puff, a room of my own and I was in business. I was giving it to my mates to sell and we were shovelling in the profits. Puff was worth more than gold in prison. But I got them to charge the same price as you would pay on the outside – £10 for an eighth of an ounce. I was trading it for phone cards, tobacco, clothes and jewellery. I soon had a drawer full of goods, a Chanel suit (handy for court appearances) and the latest trainers too. The inmates I traded the puff with would pay by getting their relatives to send me gear through the post. It was a nice little arrangement. All because of the big lump of puff I got inside by thinking ahead before I walked into court that day.

Well, I was doing pukka. When the doors were opened each day, my cell was packed with inmates and I wasn't even the one who was selling it. My mates were. There was a group of us hanging around together by now. They even included Sharon – my gypsy pal from East Sutton Park, who had turned up at Cookham

Wood – and we all had a right laugh. The whole wing was happy. Puff didn't hurt you and, believe me, everybody's world in prison looked a bit dark. Who could blame us for turning the lights up?

The authorities allocated me a job in what we called the sweat house. You had to machine-stitch 150 pairs of prison jogging bottoms a day for £7 a week and, for every 10 pairs you completed above that, you earned an extra penny. Well, I told my mates that the prison wasn't getting one pair of from me and I just broke the machine when nobody was looking, by breaking the sewing-machine needle. They moved me to another machine and I broke that as well. At last, the woman who was running the shop – a civilian – told me I wasn't very good at machining and put me on a third machine.

'This is my baby,' she said, stroking the machine.

'I won't be able to work it,' I said but she insisted and put me on it. You know what? I broke that one too. I swear, I thought she was going to cry but I had warned her. I told myself I was a prisoner and not a slave and I didn't feel too bad about it. I swore they wouldn't get one pair of jogging bottoms out of me and they didn't. She wouldn't have me back in the sweat shop after that, thank God, so my mates got me a job with them earning £10 a week working for the prison electrician. We sat in a hut all day listening to music, reading the papers, drinking tea and coffee and all we had to do was change the odd light bulb. In prison, it wasn't what you knew, it was who you knew – believe me. But it was all too good to be true and eventually me and my mates were called to the office one day and the senior officer said he knew what we were up to.

'You two are selling marijuana for her,' he said, pointing at us in turn. Well, we had been grassed. We denied it all the way. My two mates were pukka. I must say, nearly everyone in that prison was. Some weren't but you'll hear about them later and, at this moment, everyone was proper and the two I was with were the best.

'Look, sir, just because were being good girls, you have to blame it on drugs, don't you?' one of them said to the officer. 'It's us, sir, not drugs, that is keeping us mellow and happy. We are good girls now. We don't want riots or fighting. We just want to be good girls and I swear we don't know anything about drugs. It's just us being good.'

I was trying so hard not to laugh and it was killing me. I mean, we didn't want to upset this officer and piss him off but he just burst into laughter and threw us out of his office. I was screaming with laughter at what happened. Then my mate said, 'Jane, puff makes us mellow and they know it. While we're all puffing, we're all happy and I just told him, if he wants to nick us and start fucking with us and making us take piss tests to check for drugs, we're going to start rioting – but in a girly, respectable way. There hasn't been any trouble on this wing since you arrived and they know it. They aren't stupid. Puff's not legal but it's not bad. We're not rubbing their noses in it. On the other wings it's full with heroin and, believe me, Jane, they are having wars to deal with over there.'

It made sense and I understood. It was sweet in Cookham Wood. Don't get me wrong, there was no place like home and nobody wanted to be in prison but we had no choice and you had to make do. It was one good prison. Even the screws were fair and treated us like humans, rather than as if we were their enemy. There was the odd wrong 'un but that was rare in this prison.

Even when I had to go on an anger management course as part of my rehabilitation, that was a laugh too. I loved it. I had to take it because I'd beaten the bird up in East Sutton Park. There were about 20 of us in the group and we had to do role-playing to help us control our anger. I loved these classes. We were in the group one day and I saw that the worst of the worst in the prison were present. The officer running the class asked me what I would do if I was at the prison medical hatch with a headache and someone pushed in. Well, I jumped up and warned the inmates that, if anyone tried to bunk in front of me, they would have more than a fucking headache. 'I'll give yous a headache, neck-ache and back-ache because I'll beat the living daylights out of the lot of you,' I said, playing up to my audience

'No, no, no,' said the course manager. 'Sit down, Jane. We're here to help you and teach you how to let people push in front of you without you losing your temper.

You need to control your rage and just let them go in front of you and keep calm.'

I wasn't having that. 'Are you sick or something?' I asked. 'This isn't a queue at Tesco with a load of housewives and little old grannies. We all know that, when the old granny bunks the queue in Tesco, you just laugh and tell her it's OK. But we're talking about the prison medical queue, where there are drug dealers, murderers, armed robbers and all the criminals in this country, and you want me to stand here and lie to them and say, "I'll let them push in and take it on the chin?" I don't think so, somehow. Do you? And as for you lot, you have been warned. If you try and bunk in front of me, you know what will happen.' I was play-acting. My eyes were blazing and I was shouting but I knew what I was doing. I was winding her up.

So then she said, 'Well, let's try something else. You go in to a pub and, when you're at the bar, you see your boyfriend in there with another woman. What do you do?'

I jumped up again. 'What, my Matt in the boozer with another bird?'

'Yes,' she said.

Well, I was on my feet now. 'I'd pull out my 9mm Browning,' I screamed, 'and I'd point it straight at him and tell him he's got one minute to convince me that she isn't with him or his brains are going to be splattered all over the wall. Then I'd get my other gun from my other pocket and make sure everyone shuts the fuck up and lets the man I worship start to talk because what he says next, his life depends on.'

'No, no, no, Jane,' the officer said.

By this time me and the whole class were screaming with laughter. Even the screws were holding their heads and laughing. 'Jane, you can't do that,' she said, getting a bit exasperated but smiling like she knew it was a big joke.

'If my Matt wants to play with fire, he knows he will get burned,' I added for good measure. 'There are no ifs or buts in this conversation, in my book. It's written in stone.' We were all laughing but I asked the teacher what she would say to her husband. 'That's OK, love, I don't mind? I'll go home and wait for you in bed. You carry on betraying me and you can even bring me home some AIDS and syphilis. I don't mind. I love it.'

But by now everyone was just rolling about. It wasn't all laughs though, I must be honest. It got sad at times in that class. We had to write a problem down with a partner and then try to solve each other's problem. I wanted to sneak Matt in for a night of passion while the girl partnered with me said she had five children and had got eight years in prison and had nobody to look after her kids. So they had all been put up for adoption. At the bottom of her note she added, 'Please help me get them back.' Tears filled up my eyes. I couldn't even swallow. I just looked at her, grabbed hold of her and we cried. In fact, the whole class ended up crying when the teacher read out her problem. I couldn't believe that, through going to prison, she had lost her kids. But when a prisoner got more than a five stretch and there was nobody on the outside to look after the children, they lost them. It was that simple. I must say, it woke me up that day. I wouldn't play that game again. Getting shot hadn't hurt me half as much as her problem did.

But, in general, everything was going OK and my 31st birthday was coming round. Matt and John were going to come to see me but there was a petrol strike on and I was getting worried because nobody was getting visits because of the strike. Even the screws weren't turning up for work. As it turned out, I never had so many cards and presents in my life as I did on that birthday. I got done up, as my Matt and my son were coming. I prayed they would make it. I would understand, I thought, if they couldn't because of the strike but, please God, make this day my day. And God answered my prayers and in they walked.

I had earlier asked Matt on the phone to get me a pair of sovereign earrings for my birthday but he refused. He said, 'You think you can leave us out here on our own, picking up the pieces, and then ask us to buy you presents? Dream on, Jane. You're lucky we come up to see you.' But that was just Matt's way. He said it with tenderness and charm. And I was lucky. Them coming to see me was priceless anyway. No number of presents could match that. We were the only people in the visiting hall and I was like a little girl at Christmas. 'I'm glad you made it,' I said.

'I wouldn't let you down, girl, now, would I?' Matt said.

'Never,' I replied. For all our differences, he never had. Yet I'd let him down so many times. We might not be together as a couple but he was still my knight in shining armour, my best friend and soul mate. What would I do without him? I thought. I said, 'I didn't think you would be able to get here because of the petrol strike.'

'I've been out nicking petrol all night just to get here,' Matt said. Well, we all screamed with laughter. It was a brilliant day. John was doing really well and looked so happy. He always made me proud. My poor son had gone through so much with me and took it all in his stride. He was a real soldier and I shone with pride at the sight of him. When it was time for them to leave, I was choked. I knew I wouldn't see them again for a while. But the visit had made me the happiest woman in the world.

'Guess who is getting the strip search at the end of this visit?' I said. 'It is usually random but, as I'm the only one with a visit, we know it's me.' I didn't mind though. There was a big difference to being strip searched in Cat A to enduring the odd random search on a visit. This was all good, in my book. I kissed them both goodbye and waved them off. After the strip search, I was taken to the reception area, where they said there was package for me. There was the biggest card I'd ever seen and a small box. Inside it was the pair of sovereign earrings that Matt had pretended he would never buy. I wanted to cry with happiness. But I didn't. I was in prison and needed to stay strong so I just screamed and ran as fast as I could back to my wing.

That night the girls arranged a surprise party for me. If I say so myself, it was one of the best birthdays I've ever had. Believe me, it was. You might think I'm mad. But let me tell you that I met some decent, loyal and safe people in prison. They wouldn't stab you in the back, set you up, grass you up or go on the enemy's side. On my birthday they made me feel so good and happy. Don't get me wrong. I would have loved to have been at home with my son and Matt and I wasn't but we made the best of it. I thanked them from the bottom of my heart.

Our wing was generally one big happy family, apart from the odd bit of bitching, which never lasted. There wasn't that much trouble in Cookham Wood as a whole. On our wing we used to hold our own court sessions, just to stop anybody getting out of hand. I was judge, my mates the solicitors and barristers and we would pick the jury from the rest of the inmates. When anyone was rowing, we'd just bring them before our own court and deal with it. It always ended up with everyone laughing and not taking it too seriously. It passed the time and lightened the mood sometimes. We got the odd wrong 'un but they didn't last long. We soon got them evicted off the wing, no bother at all.

One weekend the prison went on lockdown because

the screws were on strike. To tell you the truth, I hated it. I didn't mind being in a single cell because, as soon as my door opened, everybody came in. But when the door wasn't opening all over the weekend, it was a bit quiet and lonely. In those days we didn't have televisions in our rooms and I'd already read virtually the entire library. Well, when I say the entire library, I mean Martina Cole, the fiction writer who writes about gangsters – and especially female gangsters – from the East End. *Dangerous Lady* was one of my favourites, even though I read loads of her other books. But I've got to tell you, Martina, my life has been crazier than any of your characters and I'm not a work of fiction. Lynda La Plante and Patricia Cornwell were my other favourites. I read loads of their books. It was mad though. I'd never read a book in my life until I went to prison.

I decided I didn't like being on my own in a cell and doubled up with my friend Sharon, by now my best mate. She was working in the laundry and it had got a bit much in there. She had hundreds of women's clothes to wash. Some wanted it done one way and some another. I don't know how she coped with all the women bitching about how they wanted their washing. So I told her to do it all the same way and say that, if anyone had special requirements, they should do it themselves. She couldn't stand the moaning she got from them, she told me, and she was worried she would lose her job because of it.

'No, you won't,' I told her. 'If they want their clothes washed in a different way, they can do it themselves or it won't get done. Tell them that.' So she did. One day we were lying on our beds when the door flew open and a skinhead bird with a few of her mates told Sharon to get outside, as her top had shrunk in the wash and she was not happy. I just jumped up, grabbed the bird by the throat and warned her that, if I ever heard her talk to my mate like that again, I would do her.

'You are one of nearly four hundred women whose clothes this girl has to wash and, if anything's going to shrink, don't fucking put it in there. Wash it yourself by hand,' I told the skinhead. Well, baldy wasn't so brave anymore. 'If you want to pay her for giving your washing the special treatment – like a few other people do – and she agrees, that's fine. But for now, you had better apologise to her before I batter you for piling into our room like you own the place.'

Her mates had already done a runner and left her on her own and this bird was now shitting herself and begging gypsy Sharon for forgiveness. But Sharon wasn't having it and told her to get lost and learn some manners. Good on her.

Another time I was coming back from a visit with Dad when I came across one of the inmates from another wing doubled up on the floor. I picked her up and asked what had happened. She told me she had been 'de-crutched' but that she was alright. Then we went our separate ways. Now, I'd never heard of being de-crutched so I asked my mate what it meant and she told me. I was not amused. In fact, my blood was boiling. Believe me, the Gran just turned up for the first time in a long time. Being de-crutched meant that this girl had been held down by two inmates while a third stuck her hand up her crotch to see if she had any drugs up there. She had just come from her visit when they pounced. In my book, that's called rape. These sick inmates sexually assaulted this girl and I wanted to know who they were because, if they thought they were getting away with that, they were mistaken. It didn't take long before I found out who all three of them were.

I battered each and every one of those dirty, filthy nonces. I thought I had been around but I had never heard of anything like that before. It didn't happen on our wing and, although I wouldn't usually get involved in the troubles of other wings, I thought this was a prison thing and it wasn't happening while I was in here. Over my dead body. And it didn't. I made examples of those three and it soon got round the prison that I had battered them.

I found time to put my sentence to some good use and get some education. So I signed up for English, maths and computer studies and, you know what? I loved studying and passed with flying colours – NVQ levels 1 and 2 in English, maths and computers. I'd never really had an education. I mean, when I was supposed to be at school, I was out doing armed robberies but I decided it was better late than never.

But now it was time to move on. I'd been in this prison nearly a year and, although it was the best I'd ever been in, I needed to be thinking about home leave and I couldn't do them here so my aim was to get back to an open prison. I needed to get a move on. I could only get one home leave visit a month and I could claim them after I had done half my sentence. I put in an application for a transfer and, because I had done courses in anger management, reason and rehabilitation, I was allowed to go back to East Sutton Park. I was sad to leave all my good friends at Cookham Wood, especially gypsy Sharon. We were so close but I had to think about myself and getting home and being back looking after John. I went back to East Sutton Park with a few other people and there were others from Cookham Wood who had got there just before us, so I was well pleased.

I went straight on to doing a catering course to help me get a job on the outside because I had decided I wanted to go straight for the first time in my life. I loved the course. I worked eight hours a day for five days a week and passed NVQ levels 1, 2 and 3. Now I had something to show for my time locked up.

I began home leave and my first 12-hour visit was mad. My brother picked me up and we drove past an Essex pub, which had been taped off with yellow tape used by the police at scenes of crimes. It looked like something serious had happened there the night before. We reached my house and my John was waiting for me.

He was so excited to see me and there were a few tears and a lot of hugs. Then some of his mates turned up looking worried. I asked John what was going on and he told me that him and his mates had been to that pub the night before and there had been a big row. He said it didn't have anything to do with him but he got dragged into it when a coke dealer in the boozer threatened him. John said he didn't understand why this bloke turned on him and I believed him.

He said, 'I thought he liked me, Mum, but when it kicked off, he turned on me in the car park. So I picked up a brick and hit him with it. It took his ear off, then his mate come at me and I done him as well. A couple of them ended up in hospital and now all their crew are coming after me with guns. My mates have said their wives have got together to talk about what their husbands are planning to do to me.'

Now I knew why the pub was taped off and I was not amused by these fucking coke dealers. Another bunch of Essex boys. Well – they were actually men and my boy and his mates were kids. John was still only 16 and these men were in there 30s. I could have done without this grief on a day out of prison but it was my boy and it needed sorting. 'Don't worry,' I told John, and I went to dig up my guns. They were well hidden somewhere nearby. Armed with my Browning pistol and my 9mm automatic, I went to find the wives. They didn't expect to see me at their get-together. I pulled out my gun. 'Get your fucking husbands here now,' I said. 'Anyone who thinks he can harm my boy is going to get buried today.'

They started panicking because they knew they were dealing with the Gran and, unlike Jane, she had zero sense of humour. So they phoned their blokes and told them to come over. As they arrived, I got them all at gunpoint. I'd got guns in both hands and I told them that my boy was off limits. 'If anyone lays one hand on my boy, I'll wipe their name from the fucking phonebook,' I said. 'So who's the big fucking gangster who's going after my boy?'

It was pure fear on their faces. They were out of their depth and they knew it. They could not believe how far I was prepared to go and they could see from my eyes that I meant every word. 'I will blow yous all away here and now,' I said as they stood there shitting themselves.

They soon begged me to 'calm down, calm down'.

'I've been in prison for over a year,' I said. 'I come out for a day and my son's at war with a load of fucking wannabes. Just because you sell coke, you think you're gangsters. Picking on kids... you should be ashamed of yourselves. Well, let's see how fucking brave yous are.'

They quickly agreed and said they shouldn't be arguing with John but looking out for him instead. 'We don't want to fall out with you, Jane,' one said and everything calmed down. I went home with their promise to leave John alone.

It was lucky I was home that day. I let them apologise but I warned that, if I found out that anyone said so much as a bad word to my boy, I would go after them and they wouldn't get a second chance. I put my guns back in their hiding place and spent the last few hours with my son. And it turned out to be a good day after all. I told John to keep away from pubs because what had happened scared me. Yet I also knew I wasn't setting him the greatest example.

When it was time to go back to prison, I was very sad but I knew John would be OK now, as each and every one of those blokes from the pub had phoned him and apologised. They even offered him their help if ever he needed it. So my mind was at peace when I went back inside. Or as much as my lifestyle would allow.

When I got back, all the other girls who had visits were in the TV room discussing their day. When I walked in, they asked me how my leave had gone. 'What did you get up to, Jane?' one asked.

'I went to war,' I said. 'My boy was having a bit of trouble so I sorted it.' I think they thought I was joking. I had to laugh myself. That was the way my life was. My first visit home in over a year and I had to go to war but at least I won, so it was all good.

I had only got a couple of months left to serve and was well excited at the thought of going home. I phoned John every day to make sure everything was OK before being released in August 2001 after serving 16 months – half of my sentence. I was so happy to be back with John and to look after him properly. I thank God that, when I got home that day, he was in one piece and as healthy and strong as ever. By now he was a strapping six-foot-tall young man. He was 16 but he was a man. He had taken everything that life and I could throw at him and come through strong. I pledged there and then that I would go straight for the rest of my life.

PART THREE

IT ALL TURNED EVIL

12

GOING STRAIGHT

In the straight-and-narrow world
I was being robbed blind.

I was home and found that, not only had the bills been paid but my dogs were healthy and John had even managed to save ten grand. A lot of men can't survive in today's world but my boy had not only survived but turned a profit.

Matt stayed around for a while because he was so used to helping out John. But one day he said he was going away and we said our goodbyes. He encouraged me to go straight before he went. He didn't want to see me inside again so I promised him I would stay out of trouble. And, believe me, I really meant it because I'd had enough. I so wanted a normal life. I prayed for things to get boring, believe it or not, because I knew John and I needed that sort of stability.

GYPSY JANE

Now, I'd never had a proper job but I had some qualifications from prison and I thought I might have a chance. I applied for a job as an assistant manager in a coffee shop. They didn't ask about my convictions so I kept quiet and got the job. I absolutely loved it from the start, even though it was actually costing me money to go to work. Each week, when I was signing on, I got £100 rent, £25 council tax and £70 living expenses for a total of £195. Now I was taking home £180. Take off the £100 rent and £25 council tax and I was left with £55 – down £15 a week. But it didn't matter because, at last, I felt like somebody. I felt like a normal person and it was such an honest and good feeling. It was funny because armed robberies as a 14-year-old girl had made me feel like somebody. Now things had turned full circle.

Going straight wasn't as easy as you might think it would be, not when you come from a background like mine. One of the managers in the coffee shop was bad news because he was never there. Yet he put down on the wage sheets that he was doing 12 hours a day, 6 days a week, when it was unusual for him to be in for an hour a day. I was doing all the work with the other staff. He was a miserable man, who picked on the others, and I grew to hate him. I didn't care that he wasn't there, as it was a happier place without him. The truth was, though, he was fiddling the owners out of thousands of pounds and I just turned a blind eye because I'm not a grass.

I wasn't tempted to do the same thing. I loved my job and my new life. I was home every night for John and I wasn't worrying about being nicked or anything like that. So I suppose you could say the game had changed for me. I never stole a coffee bean from that place. And that was another thing. I might have been an armed robber but, as soon as someone put their trust in me, I was proper. I was doing everything in that shop, from the wages to delivering the takings to the bank. Can you believe it? I was on cloud nine and revelled in what I was doing. Then one day I noticed £30 was missing from my purse. I told the other manager and he asked me if I knew who was responsible but I didn't. I suspected it was one of the lads who worked in the shop but I had no proof so I kept my mouth shut. I went off that boy but I didn't do or say anything.

Christmas was coming up and I had a grand with me when I went into work one day. I was going to buy John a present. I gave the bundle of cash to the other manager to put it in the safe for me until closing time when I planned to go shopping. But when I came to ask for the keys to the safe to get my money, he told me he hadn't put it away but had left it on top of the safe. Bloody hell, I thought. Luckily, it was still there – or at least it seemed to be. But when I counted it out, it was £100 short. The manager said, 'I hope you don't think I took it,' all insulted when I confronted him about it.

I said it had never crossed my mind that he would have taken it but that, now he had denied it, I knew that he had because I hadn't even accused him. He said he was going to call the police. 'Fuck the police,' I said. 'You had better call an ambulance if you have nicked my money.' How quickly things can change through no fault of your own. Oh, how I wanted to do him but I just walked out of the place that day because I knew I would have ended up back in prison for killing this man if I hadn't left there and then. He didn't call the police and I never went back to work there.

I was so gutted and, when I got home, it was hard to hold back the tears. I didn't feel like that because of the money or the manager but because of how hard I was trying. I had put in eight months' work for nothing. This so-called normal person had nicked off me and yet I was supposed to be the villain. I knew I was but this scum was worse than me because he had stolen from his own.

The next day I went straight to the Job Centre to try and get another job. That was how much I wanted to stay out of trouble. You couldn't say I wasn't trying. I was doing more than trying. I was putting my heart and soul into going straight. The man I spoke to was really nice and helpful and could see how much I wanted to work. He immediately got me another job as an assistant manager in a fast food takeaway. And it all worked out well because I was on better money. I was getting £90 a shift and I could do two shifts a day. I loved work all over again and I got my head down.

Now, I don't know what it was about the straight world but, yet again, the manager turned out to be a bully. Is there some sort of rule that says bosses can act like Nazis and the workers have to pretend to be stupid? Because that was how it was beginning to feel. This man was sending people home just for talking and stupid little things like that. I was convinced he had been bullied at school and was now getting his own back. Well, as you know by now, I hated bullies. I was working every hour I could but it wasn't long before I had a run-in with the manager. He tried to send a man home for talking, which meant his money would be docked. Now this employee had a mortgage and a family and by this time I had had enough and stood up for him. I told him to stay at work and ignore the manager because he had no right to be doing what he was doing. So the manager took it out on me instead, by changing my worksheet to make it look like I had done fewer hours than I had. Once again I had ended up being done while doing an honest job. I didn't know how people put up with this.

Again, after about six months, I had to leave the job before I did something I would regret. Who were the real criminals? I mean, what a joke! I'd gone straight and been robbed by both employers. I gave up and went on benefits. I was so fed up with it. I felt like I had more chance of getting lifed off for going straight than for anything I'd done in the criminal world, where nobody would dare to have me over. I mean, I was going to end up killing someone at this rate. It just wasn't right. In the straight-and-narrow world I was being robbed blind.

13

FRANK, TONI AND BOB

All I ever wanted to be was a nobody, living a
normal life with a loving family.

I had been out of prison for a while now and I was
going through all my old prison stuff when I came
across a letter from an old friend of mine called Frank.
He had sent me a letter and a Valentine's card quite a
while back, when I was in prison.

I was disappointed in receiving the card, as Frank
had been with a friend of mine at the time. Being a
woman of loyalty, I didn't like betrayal in any way so I
had replied to his letter and just ignored the Valentine's
card. Since being home again, I realised Frank hadn't
been with his girlfriend for a few years now. She had
made a new life with a new man and they had a couple
of kids. It was well and truly over with Frank, who was
still inside. He had got a life sentence for murder. I

understood why he had sent me the card now and wrote back to him as a friend. We had grown up together in Silvertown and he had become a good mate. Within a week he phoned me and we started to write to each other regularly.

Then there was Matt. I hadn't seen him for about a year now and I hadn't been in a relationship with him for over five years but he was still my best friend and soul mate. What he had done for John and me in our times of trouble created a bond that would last a lifetime. He had been there when I needed him the most. For that I would always be truly grateful. I would die for Matt, yet I was used to him not being around anymore. He had gone back home to Ireland and I was used to the idea of being on my own. Matt had his own life to get on with.

And so, in time, Frank's letters turned into declarations of love. He was ten years older and he had a way with words. He made me feel so special. You could say I fell in love with a letter. Frank was getting towards the end of his time and was now in Ford open prison in West Sussex and starting to get home leave. On one visit his mum had a party in Silvertown. Frank invited me and I was so nervous but I still went. It was like a blast from the past. I knew everyone there and Frank and I danced all night. It was lovely. That night Frank came home with me and slept on the settee. It was so nice and old-fashioned and in the morning his dad picked us up and we went to his parents' for Sunday dinner with all his family. John didn't come with me as he was now 18 and wanted to be with his own mates but he was pleased for me and liked Frank. He was happy that I was happy.

After lunch we had drinks, caught up and chatted about old times for ages. Then it was time for Frank to go back to prison so I went with him and his dad and dropped him off at the prison gates. It had been lovely – the first weekend I had spent with a man in many years and I was on cloud nine. At the prison gates Frank had kissed me for the first time. He caressed my face with his hands, kissed me on the lips and I just melted and fell in love.

Frank started coming home most Sundays and his dad and I would pick him up, spend the day with him and then drop him back at prison. As the months went past I fell deeper and deeper in love. Then one day, on one of his visits, we made love for the first time. I hadn't been with a man in so long and I had mixed feelings of love, betrayal and guilt. I felt I had betrayed Matt, even though we hadn't been together in over five years. I hadn't even seen him for almost two years. Yet the guilt was overwhelming. He was my soul mate and, although we were not a couple, I always felt I was still his girl. So it felt so wrong when I made love with Frank. Yet somehow I had convinced myself it was right. I seemed to need the sweet, comforting words of a loving man. So I put the guilt to the back of my mind and enjoyed the beautiful feeling of someone caring for me and loving me. Oh, how I felt good in one way and so bad in another. I had wanted to be everything Matt had wanted me to be. I just wasn't able to do it. How I wished I could turn back the clock and be all those things and avoid the heartbreak and betrayal. Oh, how I wished for that!

Then one day Frank phoned me to tell me the parole he was hoping for had come through. He was a free man and was coming home for good in the next couple of weeks. I couldn't believe it. He said he wanted to come and live with me and I started to panic. Matt would kill us both. I knew I hadn't seen Matt for a while but I also knew that, when I did, he would expect everything to be just as he had left it. That was Matt. He wanted to disappear for God knows how long and then return as if nothing had changed. But when he did come back, he would never accept another man in my life. So I told Frank, 'No.'

I said, 'I haven't signed up for this, Frank.' I realised then that I wanted to have a long-distance relationship with Frank, not a full-on relationship. I was being unreal and selfish, I knew, but if Matt found out about Frank, he would kill him. So I told Frank I didn't want to see him again. I ignored his calls and letters. I was so worried about Matt finding out and that meant it was a no-go with Frank.

Then Frank upped the emotional stakes. On one of his final home leaves he said that, if I didn't want to be with him, he was going to do a runner from prison. He threatened to go on the run there and then. I told him he had to go back or he would lose his parole. He had already done 15 years and was nearly out. I told him to think about his family. 'They have waited fifteen years for you to come home to them,' I pleaded. 'Don't do something crazy now. See sense.'

But he just said he didn't care. I felt I was the only thing on this earth at that moment that could save him from himself. I couldn't let him do it, for the sake of his family. How could I let him ruin his parole? So I agreed to let him come and live with me in Essex. It was a moment of weakness I would come to regret.

When Frank left prison, his family threw a big party in Silvertown. My dad came as well and Frank went up to him and said, 'Ron, while Jane's with me, you'll never have to worry about her again. She's safe now.'

My dad replied, 'I've never had to worry about my Janie, Frank. And now you're with her, it's you who is safe.' And, before I could stop him, he added, 'She will protect you from anyone... well, except Matt. I'm not sure on that score, son.'

Frank asked, 'Who's this Matt?'

I said, 'No one,' but Dad had already planted the seed. I took Frank to one side and told him that Matt was my ex and a very powerful man. I told him not to worry and I gave my word of honour Matt would never harm him. Well, Frank gave it the gangster bit that he would do Matt if he came for him but my dad and I just exchanged a knowing glance. Matt could deal with Frank, even if he had one hand tied behind his back and was blindfolded. By now my dad had realised he shouldn't have mentioned Matt's name.

Apart from that incident, the party went well. But I knew I had some explaining to do when we got home. I told Frank all about my relationship with Matt. But Frank just gave it the big 'un and held it against me that I had never told him about Matt. Why, I didn't know, but jealousy played a major part in his annoyance, I suppose. To be honest, it ruined our relationship. No matter how much I tried, we always rowed over it. It got so bad that it was impossible to live together, so I told Frank to move out. He got a flat in the East End. I used to go and stay at his on a weekend but our relationship became on and off – more off than on. When it was good, it was really good but, when it was bad, it was really bad. Frank wasn't the man I had known all those years ago. He had changed and we ended up having many more rows. I don't know if it was prison that changed him but those 15 years certainly hadn't done him any good. I wanted to believe we could make it but, in my heart, I knew we couldn't and we just grew further apart.

Then one day Matt knocked on my door again. He stood there with a new Alsatian dog called Baron – a gift for John – and a bunch of flowers for me. I was so excited to see him but so nervous as well. Oh, but how good it was to see my Matt – my soul mate. Within minutes it felt like he had never been out of my life. John was over the moon with his dog. It was fully trained and there to protect us. John and Matt were so close that John was as excited as me about his return. But Matt knew something wasn't right and, when I called him Frank by accident, he knew what was wrong.

I could hardly believe I had said 'Frank' but I had. I wanted to tell him calmly and break it to him gently but I had ruined that and he went mad and we started to argue and fight. I told him it had nothing to do with him but he wasn't having any of it. I said he must have had other women in the last six years but he said he hadn't. He said there hadn't been anybody since me. He had always said that, if he couldn't have me, nobody else could and at that moment in time I knew he meant it. He wanted to know who Frank was and where he lived but I wouldn't tell him. I told Matt I had given my word of honour that he wouldn't harm Frank and Matt knew I'd die protecting my word of honour. If he tried to hurt Frank, he would have to kill me too or I would kill him. That was the way it was.

At the same time, I really wished I'd never met Frank, let alone given my word to protect him. But, in my world, your word of honour was who you were and Frank was safe. Matt wanted to meet Frank and told me to get him to come over or he would go to him. I knew Matt would only have to make a phone call to find out where Frank lived if he really wanted to. If I wasn't on the scene to protect Frank, he would be in big trouble. So I agreed and, when Frank arrived, he took one look at Matt and just crumbled at the size of him. I told Frank I was back with Matt. I wasn't but that was all it took and Frank left unharmed. I was relieved the whole thing had come to a head and Matt was back and Frank was history. That was the end of Frank. I never saw him again.

So Matt was back and he was in and out like the wind. We weren't together but we were the best of friends. We were also doing a little business, doing lunch, doing dinner and, on the rare occasion he would stay, we made love. It was almost perfect. I was his, he was mine. It went deeper than any love or any passion. Not being in a couple, I was sometimes lonely but most of the time I was happy, at least to begin with. Yet, as Matt came and went as he pleased over the next two years, I began to feel lost for the first time in my life. My son was now a man of 20 and so handsome. He got his HGV licence and was working as a lorry driver. I was so proud of him. Matt did ask me to get back with him when he was around but I knew the price. He hadn't changed his dominating ways at all and, much as I loved him, I knew we would destroy each other sooner rather than later.

I had become good friends with a woman named Eileen, who I met in Rainham, and for the next few months she was there for me, And for that I thank you, Eileen, with all my heart. I was breeding Siamese cats to earn a living because I didn't want to commit serious crime. I just wanted to be like normal women. But life just didn't seem to want to let me be normal.

Matt told me he was having some trouble with the gypsies in his area down in Kent. He knew that I knew them. My gypsy mate Sharon from prison had been released and she was now the gypsy queen – the top gypsy woman in Kent. Well, in my book, she was the gypsy queen of the land. Matt knew her brother – in fact, they were best mates. I hadn't known that when I was in prison. It was a small world. Matt did some business with Sharon and it had gone wrong and turned into a war. So Matt phoned me. Being mates with Sharon's brother, Terry, he knew the last thing he wanted to do was go to war with them.

I told Matt to arrange a meet with Sharon and that I would sort it out. We met in a cafe on the M2. Sharon couldn't believe it when I turned up. It was so good to see her. I hadn't seen her since prison. She explained what was going on and I gave her my word of honour that Matt would never disrespect her but, if push came to shove, I'd die for Matt. She knew that anyway, shook hands with Matt on trust and all was well. She invited me to her place and I would have loved to have gone but Matt had other things to do and wanted to get going. Even so, it was good to see her and we promised each other that we would keep in touch. After that meeting I would say to Matt that he was powerful but, when the Irish and the gypsies went to war, I was the only one who could bring peace in both tribes. He didn't like that but he had to admit it was true.

I might have helped that time but there was far worse

to come in November 2007 and there was nothing I could do about it. Matt's cousin turned up at my place. She said, 'Jane, I don't know how to tell you this so I'm just going to say it.' She took a deep breath and I could hardly take in the words when she told me. 'Matt's dead, babe.'

My knees went weak. I wobbled and thought I was going to faint and I had to hang on to the door frame. Matt dead? He was only 42. The same age as me. 'How? What's happened?'

She told me that Ken, Matt's best mate, had shot him in the chest with a double-barrelled shotgun after they fell out over money. It was self-defence. On the night of 17 November Matt had gone round to Ken's house to sort out the money and that was when it happened. But that wasn't all. 'You have a right to know this, Jane, so I'm going to tell you the rest,' she added. Matt has had another two women on the go that he never told you about. One has just had a baby and he had been with the other one on and off for seventeen years.'

I couldn't believe what I was hearing. I was in shock but, instead of grieving, my mood turned into anger. This might sound mad but in the space of a few moments my love for Matt turned to hatred. He had been my soul mate – my everything. But now it seemed I didn't even know him. If he had still been alive, I would have killed him myself. Everything I believed had been a lie. Matt's cousin suggested I sit down but I told her to leave, as I wouldn't be responsible for my actions.

I had the hump with her because of the way she had told me. She hadn't spared me at all. In one breath she told me he was dead and that he had betrayed me for years.

I don't know how I got through the next few days. John knew I was upset and he was grieving too. I tried not to trouble him. My mind was in turmoil. I should have been grieving but I was hating.

Then, about a week later, Sharon turned up at my door. She explained to me that the other women, Phoebe and Tracey, knew about me and each other. Phoebe, who had the baby, was terrified of me so I told her to bring her to me and to tell her that she had nothing to fear from me. That night she brought 29-year-old Phoebe with her one-year-old baby son, who was named Matt. The boy was the spitting image of Matt and I fell in love with the baby and felt so sorry for Phoebe. My heart went out to her. She was so terrified that it hurt to see it. She thought she couldn't go to Matt's funeral because I would do her if she did. I said, 'I only just found out Matt had two other families and a child when Matt was shot.'

I asked if Tracey had any kids with Matt. She said they didn't and I told her that meant baby Matt was going to get everything that had belonged to his dad. 'He's Matt's blood,' I said and promised to go with her to sort it out with Tracey. We arrived at Tracey's house at 3am that same morning and woke her up. When she opened the door, she knew who I was straight away. She said she hadn't been seeing Matt when he was with me and that Matt had left her. I told her I didn't give a shit about Matt any longer and that I was only there for his boy.

'Everything of Matt's goes to the baby,' I told her.

That night she signed everything over to baby Matt and agreed to deliver by the weekend. So I had done what I'd gone to do. The baby's mother was at peace and we dropped her off and I went to the gypsy site to stay for a while with Sharon. I needed to prepare for Matt's funeral and Sharon was there for me all the way. But I began to think about the other woman, Tracey. Although she didn't have any kids with Matt, she had been with him for 17 years and she did have 4 kids by another man. I know how much my own son loved Matt so I knew her kids must have loved him as well. I decided to go back and see her alone.

I could see this woman was hurting, even as she tried to reassure me that Matt had finished with her by the time he had got together with me. I told her I wasn't there about Matt. I couldn't care less about him at that time. I was there to make sure she was OK. In any case, she didn't know that saying that Matt had finished with her only made it worse for me. I would never want another woman's man. I'm not like that and it hurt me to hear her say that. She said I was his soul mate but, again, at this moment in time I hated Matt for all the lies. I felt betrayed and didn't believe he was my soul mate.

'I didn't even know him really,' I told Tracey. 'He was

just one big lie.' How they both coped with knowing he had other women was beyond me.

I was there a few hours before I phoned the gypsies to ask them to come and pick me up. I now felt as much for Tracey as I did for Phoebe. My heart went out to both of them. We were preparing for the funeral, which was to take place near Maidstone in Kent, and I don't know what I would have done without Sharon. I decided that Matt was to be cremated and that John, Phoebe, baby Matt, Sharon and I would be in the first car and Tracey and her family would be in the second car. I didn't care who was in the other cars. This didn't go down too well with Phoebe. She didn't even want Tracey and her family there but I insisted that Tracey and her family went. It was Matt's day. She said it wasn't fair on the baby. To be honest, I'd had enough of her and I told her this wasn't about her or the baby and that she should stop using baby Matt as a weapon.

I played 'See You On The Other Side' by Ozzy Osbourne for Matt at the funeral. Although I hated Matt in my mind for what he had done, in my soul I knew I still loved him. I just didn't want to admit it. The lyrics of loss and leaving summed up my feelings perfectly. The funeral went well and, when it was over, I told both families that, if ever they needed me, I was just a phone call away. I thanked Sharon for being there for me and left Matt's ashes with Phoebe and then I left for home.

It felt good to be back. I'd been away for a few weeks

sorting out the funeral and helping both women and just wanted to get back to my own life. When I got home, a few people came to see me to wish me well and among them was a woman called Toni. She was a Scorpio, same as Matt, and I met her through another friend and liked her straight away. It was mad because, subconsciously, I thought that, being a Scorpio, she would be like Matt. I felt I'd looked to the right and buried Matt and looked to the left and met her.

I had another mate named Clare until the day I went around to Clare's house and she and her man were rowing. I was at the front door and wanted to leave but she asked me to come in. I didn't want to but I saw the fear in her eyes so I did in the hope that me being there would put an end to their arguing. Clare was trying to get him to leave but he was coked out of his head and not having it. I wasn't going to get involved so I sat at the kitchen table wishing I wasn't there as they screamed at each other. Then it got physical and he punched her in the face.

My motto was never to get involved in a domestic but I wasn't going to sit there while he beat up my friend. I jumped up and said it would be better if he left for a couple of hours and came back when everything had calmed down. He made the mistake of telling me to mind my own business. Then he went for me. Big mistake. I picked up a vase from the kitchen table and smashed it straight across his head. He fell to the floor and there was blood everywhere, the water in the vase mixing with the blood. It splattered on the walls and across the floor and the bloke screamed for Clare to help him. By then he was trying to get out of the house. But she dragged him back inside because of all the blood. It was mental. I told her I was leaving and I told her to call him an ambulance and get rid of him. Then I went. I'd done him good and proper but he'd asked for it.

Later that night I phoned Clare to make sure she was OK and she told me she was up at the hospital. She said I had been out of order and shouldn't have done her fella. As you can imagine, that made me angry and I told her that he might use her as a punch bag and get away with it but no one would punch me. Our friendship ended that day but Toni said I was right to have done what I did and she stayed my friend. Toni and I became best friends and I grew to love her like a sister. She had a beautiful family with her man Steve, who loved her with every breath that he took, and a daughter. She had the perfect family in my eyes.

Then out, of the blue, one day Toni said she had fallen for an MP. I couldn't believe it. I was just worried for her and but she said it was nothing to do with me and, to be honest, she was right. It didn't have anything to do with me so I just turned a blind eye and prayed she would come to her senses. She then eventually told me she was going out with another man. She said this bloke's dad had died and split £250,000 between his four sons. Just like that, she said she wanted the money. Her new fella would get at least 60 grand, she said. I couldn't believe my ears and put it down to wishful thinking. Yet I was having my doubts about Toni.

I met a friend I hadn't seen for a while. She told me her brother had recently had some bad luck with money and was staying at hers while he got back on his feet. We exchanged phone numbers and said we would see each other in a few days. That night her husband texted me and asked me if would I go on a date with her brother. He was Bob – a nobody. I don't mean that in a disrespectful way. I mean he wasn't a gangster or a wannabe gangster. He was just Bob. By now I was 43 years old and I'd been out with murderers, gangsters and all the madmen of life and I just wanted to be normal. So I agreed to see Bob, who was just three years younger than me.

Bob had been out of work for a few years due to coming out of a relationship. To me, he was a breath of fresh air and I was falling in love again. I had money. I was ducking and diving, doing a bit of this and a bit of that but none of the other, if you know what I mean. Nothing too heavy. Well, I had tried the straight life and it hadn't worked, through no fault of mine.

Bob stayed at mine some of the time and, after a few weeks, he wanted to sleep with me but I couldn't. It didn't feel right because I lived with John and I didn't feel comfortable. We had to find a place of our own. Bob said he had a house he had bought for £40,000 but that it was derelict and nobody had ever lived in it. It was in a bad state. There were no doors, not even a toilet, and squatters had been in too. The garden was overgrown and had been used as a dumping site. Now I had the money to fix this house up and make it our home so we started to work on it. John was 23 by now and he gave me his blessing. Bob went back to work at his dad's forklift-truck garage and I did up the house and turned it into a home. Bob didn't bring any wages home because he owed his dad some money from when he had been depressed and his dad had supported him. He was paying him back out of his wages. At least, that's what I was told. I didn't ask any questions and, anyway, I didn't mind because he was making amends and trying to get back on his feet with my help.

Bob was no longer a layabout in scruffy clothes. He was back to being a working man and started to dress well. Oh, how I fell in love with a nobody. As I said, don't take that the wrong way. I don't mean it disrespectfully. I mean, in my world, Bob was a nobody. But I was tired of that world now. I was sick of wannabes. The guns, the knives, the drugs, the gangsters and murderers. I was finally away from all the badness of life. All I ever wanted to be was a nobody, living a normal life with a loving family. Do you know what nobodies have that I'd craved all my life? Peace of mind. To me, Bob's family was the perfect family you read about in a fairy tale. I thought I had arrived at where I wanted to be, with a bloke who was on the straight and narrow.

I spent thousands on the house. It was our dream home. I put chandeliers in every room. I fitted a new kitchen and landscaped the gardens. I did it all myself because Bob was working all the hours that God sent with his dad – or so I thought. Then one day he forgot to take his phone with him to work. A message came through from his dad. If Bob didn't phone his dad, his dad would come and tell me. I didn't understand so I went to his house and asked him what was going on. His dad invited me inside and said he felt embarrassed about the situation. 'Bob hasn't been coming to work, Jane,' he told me. 'And it isn't fair on us, as we are paying all his bills and paying him his wages as well.'

I couldn't believe what I was being told. I knew Bob's wages were going to pay off his debts but, if he wasn't going to work, where was he going? I told him I got Bob up at 6am every day, cooked him breakfast and he left for work at 7am. He didn't get home until 11pm because he was working hard to pay them back and I thought the debt was being taken out of his wages.

That was when Bob's dad told me the full story about how his son had worked for them since he left school and then got the house for £40k. He had put down £10k as a deposit before his life started to fall apart. He had taken first a £50k loan, then another £25k out on the house. Bob broke up with his girlfriend and went into a depression until I met him. They said he was doing well until the past few weeks, when he stopped going to work.

I promised them that I would sort it out and they would never have to pay another bill of Bob's. I promised to take over his debts personally and promised that Bob would be back to work the next day. When Bob came home that night, I confronted him. He gave me a story and even though it sounded far-fetched I wanted to believe him. I had put everything into this relationship and my dream was now looking like a nightmare. I just didn't want to accept that things could be so bad. So I believed him. I accepted he had been going to work and doing his best. He said he had been going to work and his dad was wrong. For some reason, I believed him.

When people used to ask me what I saw in Bob, I'd say that, in my lifetime of war, I'd finally found peace. Well, that was just a fantasy. Evil was now entering my life from a man who was a nobody. This innocent and pure man was to be my ruin. He was the biggest traitor I'd ever met but at this moment in time I chose to believe him because I didn't know what was going on behind my back. I ended up offering to take over his debts. I even thanked Diane for everything she had done for Bob and told her to send over details of his debts. When she did, I saw that nothing had been paid off of his £115k debt. But I just brought the payments up to date with my own money and put everything back on track. I told Bob to bring his wages home every week. He got £400 a week and I went halves with him on all the bills. He was left with £200 and I made sure the right amount went into his account to pay his massive debts and the weekly bills. Life seemed to be OK for a couple of months.

Then one day Bob phoned me and said he had gone to the bank to get a tenner out and there was no money in his account. I told him he was mistaken, as I had receipts for £1,700 that had been paid in but he just repeated that there wasn't a penny in the account.

'Get a printout or don't come home,' I told him and put the phone down. The statement showed that someone had been taking money from our bank in Elm Park, where I had made deposits, and also from a branch in Epping, where Bob's dad's firm was. I was furious but he made out he didn't know anything about it. I wasn't stupid though and I told him we were going to the bank together the next day to ask what had happened. 'Whoever took this money out has a card and they will be on CCTV so the bank security team will get to the bottom of it,' I said. And that was all I needed to say.

In desperation, he said that whoever had done it must look like him. I might have been gullible after the first time Bob lied to me but I wasn't having it again. I didn't want to hear more so I threw him out, there and then. As I went through the bank printouts, I could see that no bills had been paid and that in three weeks Bob had taken out £1,700. As fast as I was putting it in, he was taking it out again. Bob had £200 a week for himself but he had never seemed to have any money. Yet he never even bought so much as a fag because I used to buy them and anything else he needed. I phoned his dad and asked him to come and explain what was happening. I was in war mode now. For the first time in a long time, the Gran made an appearance.

Bob's dad couldn't believe what he saw, as I wasn't Jane any longer. I was in full combat gear with two samurai swords and I was ready for a war. People had been lying to me and I was not happy. I explained to Bob's dad that I knew what had been going on and why Bob wasn't turning up at work. He sat and listened, not only with great interest but also with fear. He asked me what I was going to do about it all and I told him. I was going to our money back.

He agreed and left. He had never seen me like this before and I could see by his face that it worried him. He must have thought I had lost it because he got back to his house and sent all the women in his family away for a week's holiday at Weymouth with his mother-in-law. Meanwhile, I continued to prepare for war. It was Friday and I took my swords to everyone I thought might know what Bob had been doing and put the fear of God into them. I wanted revenge. It wasn't just the money. It was the thought that someone had gone against me. Believe me, I only had one thought in my mind – they were going to pay!

I had gone out searching for the evil that was the root cause of the problem. After my rampage I got home and lay down on the settee. I was shattered. Bob's family didn't even phone me to see if I was OK. Not that they needed to but it would have been nice to think they cared. I mean, I was out at war with drug dealers for this family, putting my life on the line while all the women were off on holiday being protected from it all. I just took off my war gear, had a bath and waited until the morning before going back to the garage to confront them all. As I walked in, his brother said, 'Hello,' and I replied, 'Get in the office now. We're having a meeting.'

Bob, his brother, his dad and I moved into the office and I confronted them. Bob just had his head bowed. I still thought he had just got back on his feet and I really believed he was a good man with a good soul. I was heartbroken but, once again, I blamed someone else for what my man had done and I took Bob back. More fool me. Not only that but I was confiding in Toni. She was my best friend and I told her everything. Something else I would live to regret.

So Bob and I were together and he went back to work again and I was just praying that everything would be OK. All my money had gone into the house but I had a feeling that it was all slipping away. And yet I tried so hard to get our relationship back on track. I was trying to be happy again. Having blamed his brother for Bob's slide, after a few weeks I even decided to go and make amends. I asked Toni if she wanted to come to Bob's firm with me for the ride. She got all done up and off we went.

I knew it wasn't fair to keep blaming everyone else for what Bob had done but I didn't dream that this was the day Toni had planned to shatter my world in two. I had begun to realise she would try something. But I swear, as God is my witness, I truly didn't dream that Bob would play along. At this point I was just trying so hard to put our lives back on track.

We started doing the things we loved. I took Bob to the fair and to a Harrods' sale in London. I'd never been to Harrods before and it had been one of my dreams.

On Valentine's Day we went to see the queens of lovers' rock, Caroll Thompson and Janet Kay, live at the Indigo in London. We were finally living our dreams and I got a membership to the Ministry of Sound as well. I was not a clubber but Bob liked to go out. I was more of a home person but I thought the Ministry of Sound would be perfect. It is a nightclub with the most amazing disco. Bob was still doing really well. He was off the coke but he was never home because he was working hard, sometimes until midnight. As much as I tried to get him to get in earlier, he said his dad just kept loading him up with work.

One day I invited Bob's mum and dad to dinner. I cooked a lovely roast and made a trifle for dessert. It was a lovely day and, as we sat down, Bob's dad said he wanted to retire and leave Bob and his brother the firm. Now, I couldn't believe what I was hearing. I said, 'Are you joking? You want to give them your firm? Are you mad?' I was being straight. I said he had built his firm from nothing and, if they left it to Bob and his brother, I'd give it six months before they didn't have a firm anymore. I told him Bob wasn't ready for that. I cared about his mum and dad and I knew this was a bad idea so I told them the truth. Bob didn't like what I was saying but I didn't care. His mum just wanted to get rid of the firm but I warned them not to. My biggest mistake came afterwards, telling Toni all about the dinner conversation and the family plans for the firm.

I carried on trying to be happy and one day I booked me and Bob a day and night out at a boat party on the Thames. From 5pm to 11pm we would have a meal on the boat as it went up the river and then we would move onto the Ministry of Sound for an all-nighter, finishing at 7am. I was so excited to be letting my hair down for the first time in ages and so was Bob. It was on a Saturday and Bob had to work until 1pm so I told him to be home by about 3pm so it would give us a couple of hours to get to the boat in London.

Well, when 3pm came and Bob wasn't home, I phoned him but got no answer. So I called the firm and still got no reply. Time ticked on... 4pm, 5pm... and I was still sitting waiting, my best gear on. Now we'd missed the boat party. I was gutted. I kept trying his phone but there was still no answer. Six... seven... eight... nine o'clock came and went. I couldn't believe what Bob was doing to me. I felt so unhappy. This day had been planned for a couple of weeks and it had cost me a few hundred quid. Bob had ruined it. I was at the end of my tether. What should have been a great day was turning out to be a truly awful day. I phoned Toni but there was no answer from her either so I texted her and told her Bob hadn't turned up. Now, she knew I had planned this day and that it was special for me. She even said she would love a day out like that herself. I asked her in the text if she wanted to come to the Ministry of Sound with me to save what was left of the day. I told her Bob didn't deserve it and he didn't even look like showing up anyway. She texted me back but she said she couldn't come because she was at her mum's.

I was gutted. It was 1am when Bob came in. I told him he had ruined the day and, before he could start making excuses for where he had been, I told him I was still going to the Ministry of Sound. I told him he could come if he wanted to and he agreed. I was so angry but didn't want the day to be a complete disaster so we set off. I had bought him an Armani suit for the occasion and had even paid for us to be VIPs.

We didn't get there until 4.30am because Bob couldn't find the place. I was fuming. This day should have been one of our best but it was turning out to be the worst. Even so, when we got inside, my mood improved. The atmosphere was good and we both started to smile for the first time that day. We went into one of the VIP rooms and it was packed out and pumping.

Some bloke then started eyeing Bob up. 'Look at him, Bob,' I said, pointing to the bloke. 'He fancies you.' We both laughed and moved away and stood in between two dance stands by the fire exit, as I liked to have my back to the wall so I could see everything that was happening. I told Bob to go and get us a drink while I danced to the music and started to have a lovely time at last. The heat in the club was overwhelming and I felt like I was going to faint. A couple of blokes asked me to dance but I told them, 'No, thank you.' I wasn't like that. Bob was my fella, for better or worse.

It had been nearly an hour and Bob was still not back. It was packed and I knew the bar was busy but, even so, I was thinking, Where is he? There was a group of Bosnians beside me and one of the girls in the group offered me a drink. I think she could see I was struggling with the heat. But I refused, not knowing who they were. I mean, I didn't want to accept a spiked drink. You couldn't be too careful. She was in a group of about five girls and five blokes. I started to go giddy and feel faint again but they started clapping and it helped snap me out of it. Finally – after an hour and a half – Bob came back with vodka and it cooled me down. We had started to dance together when a man jumped down from a platform suspended above us and started dancing along with us. At least, I thought he was dancing with us but then I realised he was dancing with Bob and the way he was doing it was very sexual.

'Here's another bloke who fancies you, Bob,' I shouted above the music. Bob just laughed but I wasn't finding it funny by then. I was getting embarrassed so I told Bob to tell the bloke he was straight and was with me. But, again, Bob just laughed. So I told the bloke myself. 'I hope you're not trying to pull my man. He's with me,' I said politely. Well, he just moved closer to Bob, gave it a bit more dirty dancing and I exploded. I grabbed the man around the throat and ran him back to the dance platform, where he crumpled to the floor.

'Fuck off, you little poof,' I said and left him there in a heap on the floor. I have nothing against gays – I believe in live and let live – but I didn't want anyone trampling on my territory. When I got back to Bob, he was laughing.

'I gave you the hump there, didn't I?' he said

I told him that fighting off other women would make me proud but fighting a man off didn't amuse me. Then I saw them all coming. This man I had just flattened was with the group that had offered me the drink and now they were signalling to another man on the opposite stage and he was signalling another group. I knew it was going to kick off. I told Bob to shut his mouth as I had bigger problems now. It looked like half the club was with this guy but I could tell that the man on the other dance platform was the main man. By now everyone was looking at me and pointing. So I went to the main man. I'd got a knife down the back of my jeans and I screamed, 'If today's the day I die, it's a good day to die,' and I waited for his reaction. I knew that, if it went off, I was going to lose this one. There were too many of them but I'd take a few of them with me. The man signalled something to the three blokes who were homing in on me and they turned around and grabbed the bloke who had been trying to pull Bob and brought him to me. The man said he didn't know Bob was with me and I accepted his apology. I had no choice really.

It was now 6am and everyone went back to dancing. I was making out I was having the time of my life but I wasn't really. I didn't want to be there but I couldn't lose face so we stayed for the last hour. But I was gutted that Bob had put me in that position. All he'd had to do was say he was straight and with his missus but he hadn't. He had ruined everything again. What kind of man would do that to his woman? I just didn't understand.

When we left that morning, the men and women in the group I'd had the encounters with hugged and kissed me as we said our goodbyes. I danced out of there, lying, because I said I had had the time of my life but that was so far from the truth.

When we reached the car, I went mad at Bob. I asked him if he was gay. He said he wasn't but I had seen in films that gays attract gays and, believe me, they were all Bob had attracted in the two and a half hours we were there. I couldn't believe what Bob was doing to my head and, when we got home, I made him sleep on the settee.

When I told Toni about our big night out, she couldn't stop laughing. 'Do you think my Bob is gay?' I asked.

'No way, Jane,' she said. 'It was just one of those things. Don't worry about it.'

After a few days Bob and I were back on speaking terms. But I was starting to wonder about our relationship and all the stuff that had happened. Debts, coke and gays. None of it was right. Then one night I was waiting for Bob when Toni turned up. She'd got on a mini-skirt, no knickers and she was laughing about it. I didn't find it funny.

'What are you coming round here like that for,' I asked her. 'If my Bob was home and he had looked at you like that I would have gone mad.'

She knew he wasn't in and I wondered how? He was a couple of hours late so, if anything, she should have expected him to be in. I told her to go and never to come back dressed like that again. She promised she would never do me wrong but then she had previously told me she went with other men to get money. I said, 'You do your own family wrong, girl.' I knew now I wouldn't trust her as far as I could throw her. And yet I still had to trust that Bob wouldn't cheat on me with Toni, although I was growing more and more suspicious.

But it came to a head when she was over some time later, crying her eyes out after a row with her fella. At first, she said she wanted him to move out because she couldn't stand being with him. But it was Bob who stood up for her and said that all this rowing was not fair on Toni. He suggested that her bloke Steve should move in with us, in the spare room, for a few days so that she could get some peace and quiet. 'Are you mad, Bob?' I shouted. 'Why would I let her man come and stay here? She wouldn't be able to come round here herself and I would never see her.'

There was something not right going on here but for some days I just couldn't see what it was. Then the penny dropped and I became convinced he was seeing Toni behind my back and that they had both been playing me for a mug. How could I have been such a fool? I confronted Bob, but he denied it. 'I have spent every penny I had on you and this house!' I screamed, knowing I had made the biggest mistake of my life. After my endless wars, I thought I'd at last found peace with this man. What a fucking joke that was now. A sad, sad joke. 'I'm fucked now, Bob, because I have put everything into our relationship,' I said. I made him write out a receipt for £30,000 so that he couldn't sell the house without paying me back what I had put in. I just didn't know what else to do.

I found out that Bob still hadn't paid any of the bills. I lost it, big style, got a sledgehammer from the garden shed and I smashed his truck to pieces. I smashed every window, every door, every light, everything. He was just lucky I didn't take the hammer to him because I had never felt like doing anyone more in my life. When I had destroyed his truck, I went back in the house, gasping for breath, a cold fury in my eyes and an aching in my heart.

'Leave now, Bob.' I held the heavy hammer tight. 'Leave now,' I repeated, 'before I do something we will both regret.' And, for the first time in a long time, Bob did the right thing. He even closed the door behind him as he left. I slumped onto the settee. It was the worst moment of my life. I looked up to the heavens with tears in my eyes and thought about my Matt – a real man –

and wondered what I was going to do now. I was so unhappy and alone. My dreams had become nightmares, my happiness had turned to sadness and my love had become shame. I couldn't cope. I was losing this battle for happiness with every beat of my heart.

I went to bed and that's where I stayed for the next few weeks. Thank God for my son. He looked after me, brought me food and walked my dogs. I was an emotional wreck. In all my life I had never been so low. I was like a zombie, just lying in bed with my two dogs and the cats around me. My John came every day and kept begging me to snap out of it. 'This isn't you, Mum,' he would say. 'Pull yourself out of it and come back home. Don't be like this, Mum.'

But I just couldn't move. I was so wrapped up in my own misery. My poor boy had never seen me like that before and it frightened him. He kept saying everything would be OK but he didn't know what was wrong with me because I couldn't open up to him. He was my boy and I couldn't tell him about Bob. I was too ashamed. As parents, we protect our kids. I didn't want to drown him in my misery. I just kept saying, 'I'll be OK.' But I was far from OK. A woman can only take so much.

I was so unhappy, my mind played tricks on me. Was it me? Was Bob really that bad? I had second thoughts and I texted him dozens of times but he blanked me. I begged him to get off the drugs and that, despite everything I'd told him, we might still be able to work at it. I asked his dad to give him my messages and I sent flowers, chocolates and even bottles of champagne round to his mum to say sorry for the position we had put them in. He had moved back in with them and they were caught in the middle. And his dad was so lovely, always keeping hold of the hope, like me, that Bob would get off the drugs. I knew, in my head, it was over but, in my heart, I was still hoping. Love had crippled me and Bob was blanking me.

I kept phoning Toni. I needed a friend. I needed her to come and tell me everything was going to be OK. But she never came. She always had an excuse and, before long, she started to blank my calls altogether. My boy told me daily it was going to be OK but I couldn't tell him what a mess I was in. I just couldn't. I started to cry and I couldn't stop. I couldn't stop thinking about Matt. Oh, what have I done? I thought. I had been so angry with Matt since he had been killed and now I needed him more than I'd ever needed him in my life. My poor Matt, I thought. Shot dead at 42. The tears came and I couldn't stop crying. I hadn't cried in years. Well, I couldn't remember the last time I'd cried.

I kept texting Toni and told her I thought I had finally started to grieve for Matt because I couldn't stop crying and thinking about him. My eyes looked like I'd been punched, they were so swollen. Toni was always crying and I texted her that I now knew she was just pretending, as she was always dolled up and there was no way she would look the way she did if she had been crying for real. At last, I texted that I was going to drive round to show her my face. I couldn't believe the way I was. I had never been like this before, ever. Still dressed in my pyjamas, I jumped into my car and drove to hers. I beeped her when I arrived but her daughter came out and said she wasn't in. I just drove back home and got back into bed. I was gutted. She could have texted me back if she wasn't going to be there.

Then, out of the blue, something told me to get up and sort myself out. I told myself that this wasn't fair on my John. He should be out enjoying his life and not worrying and looking after me. When he came round the next day, I was up and he smiled the loving smile I didn't deserve and gave me a big hug. My boy was the best son any mother could have. Despite everything I'd done and put him through, he never judged me, never doubted me and he was always there for me, no matter what. I love you so much, John. You always make me so proud.

I was up now and I took the dogs down to the river for a walk. I had my own spot on the bank where I'd go to find peace. I'd made a little opening to get away from the path and down the bank to the river's edge. I had two rottweilers and I needed both to pull me back up again because the drop was so steep. This was my place of sanctuary, where my dogs and I went for solitude. I loved it.

I was back to being me and, once more, I was pissed off with Toni. Where was she when I needed her? So I texted her yet again and she still ignored me. This time, though, I wasn't crying but boiling with rage. I thought, Some best friend. Now I'd had enough. I hadn't heard from her or Bob. I went to her house with a can of black spray paint and sprayed 'wrong 'un' and 'slag' across the windows.

She soon came out. 'What the fuck is your game?'

'What the fuck is my game? You cheeky slag,' I replied, reaching into my motor for my Maglite torch – the same type used by the police. It was massive. I grabbed it, jumped away from the car and smashed it down onto her head as hard as I could. 'That's for not answering your phone, slag!' I screamed as she ran into her house clutching her head. 'If I find out you have done me wrong, you will be a dead whore walking,' I said as she disappeared.

I knew something wasn't right and, when Bob knocked on my door not an hour later, all the pieces finally fell into place. I had been fooling myself for too long but those days were now over. After he and his family had dropped out of sight, he was suddenly back on the scene, less than an hour after I'd done Toni, asking to come back. I took him and the dogs to the special place by the river and asked him straight out if he had done me wrong with Toni.

'No way, Janie,' he said, looking pleadingly at me. But I was not convinced. I pushed him in the river and headed back to Toni's place. Steve claimed she had left him but I knew he was talking bollocks so I went home, got another tin of paint – yellow this time – and wrote on a big board opposite her flat, 'Toni fucks, sucks and grasses anyone for money.'

When Steve came out, I shouted from across the road, 'She's a dead whore walking. All she's got is time.'

He shouted, 'Oh yeah?' and started walking towards me. 'I'm going to fucking do you, you bitch.' He was 20 stone of fat and yet I had really liked him until this point. I pulled out the Maglite again and went for him.

'Come on then,' I shouted as I raised the torch above my head. All of a sudden, he wasn't so brave.

He stopped, turned around and shouted out to where I knew Toni was cowering inside, 'She's got a weapon. Call the police.'

'Call all your fucking gangster mates as well if you think it will stop me!' I screamed. 'She has been sleeping with my man and I'm going to do her. You had better get your whore insured for a lot of money and then you should fuck off on holiday if you know what's good for you.' A new calm had come over me. 'I won't be taking any prisoners. All that whore has got left is time,' I told him as I left.

His brow furrowed when I said that. He understood what I meant, all right.

14

REVENGE

The police would have to shoot me to try to save them and we would all be gone.

My life had just come to an end. Whatever time I had left was going to be used to prepare for my son's future and then I was going to send Bob and Toni straight to hell. He was a dead man walking. She was a dead whore walking. And I was a dead warrior walking because I was going with them. I knew it was over. Everything around me felt evil. Having been a woman with morals, who valued loyalty and honour, I was crushed beyond belief. My moral code wouldn't let me accept what had happened. My honour wouldn't let me allow this to go unanswered and my loyalty now belonged to my Matt, and this was when I began to grieve for him properly.

I couldn't deal with the evil that came to me and I

gave myself two more months in this world to make things right for my son and to say goodbye to my loved ones. The two were going to hell and then the heavens would open up to claim their warrior queen. I knew how I was going to die. I was going to be shot by the police again but this time they would have to kill me to try to save the traitors. I was going to die with my sword in my hand, taking back my honour and the copper who shot me would be a hero. He wouldn't hear the truth of why I was doing what was doing until I had gone, and I would have no regrets.

I now missed Matt so much and felt so guilty at the anger I had once had for him. I realised now that he had been the only true love of my life. He had never done me wrong. He was just trying to protect me from the pain I would have felt knowing he had loved others when I didn't want him. Well, I had wanted him. I just couldn't cope with him as a person and it was my choice to let him go.

All the good memories and love came flooding back and all I wanted now was to be with my Matt again. My true, undying love. I knew he was on the other side waiting for me and wanting me and I had never wanted anything more in my life than to be with him now. And I was going to be with him. I'd had enough of this world. People I loved had let me down. I'd never done anything to anyone who didn't deserve it, yet all I seemed to attract were wrong 'uns. I was blessed to have a son with the same morals and value for honour and loyalty as me. It was breaking my heart to think of leaving him but he was 25 now and it was time for me to go.

I took John for lunch to a country pub in Epping, where we had a beautiful day. We took photos of each other and then I told him it was time to meet his real dad. At first he said, 'No way,' but I said, 'I've had you for twenty-five years and it's time for you to meet him.' I didn't want to leave this world without making things right. I told John he had no choice and that he was meeting him whether he liked it or not. I think he wanted to meet him but, out of loyalty to me, he felt he couldn't. But this wasn't about me anymore. This was about him and his future and he accepted that.

We had a three-course meal at the pub, then walked into a field nearby where a big oak tree had fallen. We climbed and played like a couple of teenagers and laughed. We just enjoyed each other's company. How my son was the best thing in my life and I knew Jamie would be just as proud as me when he met him. I got in touch with Jamie's sister and left her a letter for Jamie with a photo of John and his telephone number. I put in the letter that I had never asked him for anything but that, if anything ever happened to me, John would need to know his family.

Jamie phoned John in the next couple of days and they arranged to meet. I said to John beforehand that it would be just like the moment in the *Harry Potter* book when he got his wand. He would feel a power and he would just know he'd met his dad. I was only sorry I hadn't done it before. But I did ask John when he was 15 if he wanted to meet his dad and he had said that he didn't, so I didn't push it.

Everything went well when they met. I was a bit jealous, to be honest. John didn't drink or smoke and nor did his dad. John loved boxing and Jamie now ran a boxing club. Jamie played golf and so did John. It was amazing. How could they be so alike and not even know each other? I was glad though. John now had his whole family and I knew his best qualities came from me – his moral code, sense of loyalty and honour. I soon forgot my jealousy. They got on well and it made my day.

The next thing on my list was to get John as much money as I could before I went. He wasn't going to worry about funeral costs or anything like that. I already had a life insurance policy for £50,000 so I went and got another £150,000 on top of that. I was hoping that would soften the blow when I was gone. I couldn't think about the downside of losing me. I had to look at the best.

That summer I got a letter from Bob's solicitor telling me to get out of the house within four weeks, cutting in half my planned two months in this world. I said to Bob's dad that, if he thought I was leaving my home, he was dreaming and that he shouldn't make any plans as his son was a dead man. He should get Bob insured. I also told him that I had a receipt from Bob so he couldn't sell the house before he paid me back my

£30,000. 'But it's too late for all that,' I added. 'I don't want the money. I want him and Toni dead. I'm going to die as well.'

He said he couldn't allow me to hurt his son and I told him, 'You've got no choice. But don't worry. We will all be gone – me Bob and Toni – by the end of August, so stop with the silly letters.' It was already the beginning of August and time for me to say my goodbyes and to make amends with the people I loved.

I told John I wasn't going to be around much longer. I didn't go into any details at all. I just said I wasn't well and that, when I passed, I wouldn't be in pain anymore. He accepted it like the man he was but I could see his heart was breaking with sorrow. Even though he asked a lot of questions, I told him that was all he needed to know. How it hurt me to do this to my boy but I had to. I started telling everyone I'd only got a month to live. I told some people in the world of villains what it was all about but not everyone because I was out to commit murder. Those I let in on it could be trusted. I told them Bob and Toni had done me wrong and I was going to kill them and that the police would shoot me trying to save them. But these were villains I was telling, not family or close friends. Villains understood and they all agreed with me. I told them this was down to honour.

I had heard that one of the hard faces in the East End used to do some work for Bob's dad and I made a meet with him. This was someone I had known nearly all of my life but I hadn't seen for nearly 20 years. I needed to make sure he wasn't going to get involved. I was on a mission. Bob and Toni's time was up and they would be trying to find a way out so I got the number of the face, just in case they had gone to him for help. I introduced myself as the Gran and explained that I was at war with someone he knew and needed to find out what side of the fence he was on. He said he didn't remember me.

When I asked him, 'Have you got Alzheimer's?' he said I was mad. I said I wasn't playing and that, if he wanted to get involved, I was game. He hung up on me. But within ten minutes he had phoned back and said, 'You're Janie Lee. Sorry I didn't remember,' and we arranged to meet at the Percy Ingle bakery in Canning Town later that day. There he bought me a cup of tea and I explained everything.

I said, 'I need to know you won't get involved because I've heard you worked for Bob's family.'

'Jane, you and I are family and we go way back, even if I have got Alzheimer's, girl.'

He touched my heart with his loyalty and I thanked him but I told him it was personal and that nobody else was to get involved. 'I'm going to kill them and die the warrior I am,' I said. He assured me he wouldn't get involved and I thanked him.

Things were falling into place nicely but then I had the hardest task of all. I went and told my dad I was going to die. It wasn't easy but I had to do it. I said, 'Don't worry, Dad, Matt's waiting for me.' He went white with shock. I told him I was looking forward to it and even joked with him. 'Now, if Mum was waiting for me, I wouldn't go,' I said and we both started laughing.

Then I went to see my sister Shell. I said I'd take her to the fair for the day but, when I got there, she wouldn't go. 'No way,' she said. 'Every time you ask me to go somewhere with you, something happens.'

I told her this would be the last time we would ever get to go out as I was going to die but she refused so we stayed at hers for the day instead. We had a brilliant day, chatting and drinking tea. I hadn't told Dad or Shell the truth about why I was going to die. I just said I was ill. It was better that way.

I went to Southend after I left Shell's, bought myself fish and chips and sat on the beach counting the stars. I was going over in my mind what I had left to do. I had given John back to his dad, made sure he would have enough money and said my goodbyes to Shell and Dad. I lay there smiling and then my phone rang.

'Hello, Jane. It's Frank here. I've heard things are going down with you and I just want to make sure I'm safe.'

I told him he was safe. 'You were bad, Frank, but never evil so don't worry,' I told him. 'But make amends with your family.' I hung up. I didn't want him on my mind. It had been a long time since I'd seen him and he hadn't even entered my thoughts. Then he sent me a text that seemed threatening to me. I phoned him back. 'Go to the army and get their best if you think it scares me,' I said. 'I'm sitting on Southend beach counting the stars

and now my head is banging. Do him. *Don't do him.*
Decisions. Decisions. Now, fuck off,' and I hung up
again. Within five minutes I was surrounded by armed
police. Frank, I immediately thought.

One of the cops shouted, 'Jane Lee, get up.'

I jumped up and said, 'You've got me,' and pulled out
a gram of puff from my pocket.'

I was kept in a cell all night and they charged me with
possession. I was told to appear at Southend magistrates
court on 25 August, signed the bail paperwork and got
out. I knew I wasn't going to turn up at court. I was on
a mission and I didn't have time for all this shit. They
kept my car in Southend after I was released. So Frank
had just made the last few weeks of my life a lot harder.
I phoned him as soon as I walked free that morning.

'You're fucking top of my list now,' I said.

He denied calling the police but he was the only one
in this world who knew I was on Southend beach. Now
Bob and Toni would have company because the two had
become three.

It seemed mad, planning my own death. But it felt
right. It felt right to know I wasn't going out of this
world alone and that someone was waiting for me. He
would have waited through all eternity if that was what
was needed but I was ready now. I wanted to be with
Matt more each day. 'I'm coming, Matt,' I'd say and I
could sense him waiting for me and loving me with a
passion. I thought about him every second of the day
and I had to make right what had happened. I had just

left after his funeral and I didn't really know anything about his death. It was time to sort that out.

Matt and Ken, the man who shot him, had been like brothers. They had fallen out over money and, in a mad moment, something had gone wrong and now Matt was dead and I thought Ken was going to be facing a murder charge. I believed Matt wouldn't have wanted that so I decided I was going to take the blame for Matt's death. I would go and see Ken and tell him that I'd say I shot Matt, and give him back his life. I was going to die anyway so it was nothing to me – and Ken would be free. I knew that's what Matt would have wanted. I also had to get Matt's ashes, as I knew his wish was for them to be scattered onto a race track because of his love of cars. Phoebe was keeping them in her wardrobe. I went to her place in Kent to sort that out too.

Baby Matt was now a young child of four. He was walking and talking and my heart broke. He was Matt in every way. I loved this boy. There was an attachment that was so strong and, when I sat down and spoke to him, he told me how a big man visited him and played with him at night. I told him that was his dad and the tears rolled down my face. He told me he knew the man was his dad and not to cry. He said Matt was OK and that he was teaching him how to play football. I could feel Matt's presence and what this young boy was telling me was reassuring. It was so emotional. Out of a child's mouth come no lies. He was only one when Matt had died. His mum was freaked out by her son speaking to

Matt and she told me she had known about it for a long time. It scared her because it had to be Matt's ghost. It was weird but that is what little Matt said and his mum said it was true.

I had come to get Matt's ashes as well as see them both and say my goodbyes. I explained that I was going to die and I had to fulfil Matt's wishes that his ashes were scattered on a race track. I also told her that, when I died, I wanted my ashes to be scattered with Matt's. I said John could throw mine from one side of the car onto the track and little Matt could throw his dad's from the other. Phoebe asked how long I had left and I told her three weeks. She couldn't believe it. I didn't tell her how I was going to die. I just made her think I was ill. It was too much for her to understand.

I told her I needed to see Sharon and she drove me to the gypsy site where she lived with her husband Clint. Sharon, the gypsy queen, had always been there for me when I needed her and I needed her now more than ever. Sharon was the one person in this world to grant my wishes, as I needed my funeral to be prepared. Time was running out. Oh, how I loved my gypsy queen. What would I have done without her? Those friends of mine I called the gypsy queen and king were of a rare breed. Their friendship was unconditional. No matter what I'd done or would have to do, these people were behind me a hundred per cent with a love that broke all the boundaries. I worshipped the ground they walked on and loved them with all my heart. It was so good to see them again. I immediately told them I only had three weeks to live and not to worry.

'Matt is waiting for me,' I said but they cried. I had expected it but I didn't realise how much it would affect the people who loved and cared about me. I had to put their minds at rest. I told them I was ready and that I was even looking forward to it. They wanted to know why I was dying but I just said, 'Don't worry, it's not catching and I won't be in pain anymore.' That was all I could tell them and I asked them to be strong. I told them I needed to see Ken and that I needed them to arrange my funeral. They didn't understand but I told them I was the happiest I'd been since Matt had died. 'I'm now at peace so please don't make this any harder than it is,' I said. 'I've got three weeks and I want it to be perfect, not sad.'

'You're not going to see Ken. He killed Matt,' Sharon said, concern written all over her face.

'I know,' I said. 'But I need to know what went on.' I didn't tell them I was planning to take the blame for Matt's death. But something didn't feel right. They had a hatred for Ken in their eyes that didn't match the intensity of my own feeling. Clint said he would only tell me where Ken was if he could come with me. 'No,' I said. 'I need you to drop me off. I have to see him alone. Listen – and listen good. This is not about you being worried and protective over me. I need to see him and I'm going alone. Don't forget that I'm the Gran and Ken's the one who's hurting.' I persuaded them that there was nothing to worry about. Clint drove me to Ken's yard and then, reluctantly, drove away.

I knew something wasn't right as soon as I hit the yard. The feeling of sadness was no longer inside me. It had been replaced with a sensation that something here was very wrong. I must have known in my subconscious that things weren't right, as I was in full combat gear. I'd never met Ken. I'd only spoken to him on the phone. Matt had often phoned Ken for advice. They were best friends and, when me and Matt argued, he would always phone Ken for backup. Ken would always make Matt right and me wrong. Now I was to come face to face with him. I didn't like what I felt as I met him at the garage itself. I had come down here to meet this man as Jane but the Gran had already taken over.

He said, 'Can I help you?'

I said, 'Yes. I'm the Gran and we need to talk.' He took me into his office and I could see the fear and panic in his eyes. I told him to make me a cup of tea and explain what went on between him and Matt. 'I'm not going to be around very long and what you say now, Ken, will decide your destiny,' I told him, keeping my eyes on his. He started stuttering. I was calm and listened to what he had to say and he let down his guard. It was the biggest mistake of his life. He said Matt had deserved what he got. He started to act flash. It felt like he thought he was somebody special because he had killed Matt. I hated him for it.

'I came here knowing I'm going to kill three people,

Ken,' I told him in an icy voice. 'Then I'm going to die myself. Now I'm going to kill four people because you have just gone to the top of my list.' He didn't say a word.

One of his mates, also a friend of Matt's, was in the yard. He drove me back to the gypsy site and, on the way, he told me what had happened the night Matt died. Ken had shot Matt in self-defence. I said I didn't like the way Ken had talked about Matt and that he had got a reputation out of his death. I said all he had left was time, the same as the rest.

There was relief all around back at the site that I hadn't got into it with Ken. I put their minds at rest and I just told them that Ken was no friend of mine. They didn't know I had gone there to take the murder charge from him and had come back with another murder on my to-do list because of the way he had talked about Matt. Now there were four people who were going to hell before I went to heaven to be with my Matt.

I felt good. Now I knew what I was going to do. I had given Ken the chance to feel remorse but he had blown it and now I would regain Matt's honour and take down the man who had blown him away. A man he loved and trusted. I also found out that Ken had already faced a charge of murder over Matt's death and had been cleared. So my plan to take the blame for Ken would never have gone anywhere. He had walked free after being tried at Maidstone crown court in March, 2009 and I had just never got to hear about it. He admitted accidentally shooting Matt after Matt phoned him demanding money he claimed he was owed. The court had heard how Ken was worried that Matt was going to turn up so he armed himself with a legally owned shotgun just in case. When Matt did turn up and confronted Ken, the gun went off by accident, the court was told, and Ken was acquitted of murder. But I was judge, jury and executioner now.

I went to see Matt's other woman, Tracey. I hadn't seen her since the funeral and I said my goodbyes to her too. I had to get Matt's ashes from Phoebe as well so Sharon and I went back to her house. When we got there, she looked worried. I asked for the ashes and she started to cry and told me she no longer had them. She had buried them in the cemetery and had placed a plaque on the ground. I couldn't believe what I was hearing. I told her Matt's wishes were that they were scattered on a race track.

'Why didn't you tell me before that you had already buried him?' I asked. She said she had been too scared to keep him at her place because young Matt was talking to his ghost. I understood what she meant. She was young, she didn't really know Matt and she was thinking about what was best for her baby. I told her we had to fulfil Matt's wishes and that we would get him back. She asked how and I told her we were going to dig him back up. She nearly passed out. I could see the fear in her eyes. She was crying and saying she couldn't do it.

'This is what Matt wanted,' I told her. 'This was his

wish and, if you loved him, you would do it for him. He would hate to be buried in a cemetery.'

She agreed and I said we would go to the cemetery at midnight. I could see she was scared that someone might see us. 'Don't worry. I've got a plan. We will wear white sheets and, if anyone sees us, they'll just think we're ghosts and take no notice,' I said. I was trying to make her laugh and lighten the situation. It made Sharon amd I laugh and it did make her smile a bit – but not much.

The cemetery was pitch black that night. I lifted off the plaque and removed the earth underneath it. Phoebe said she hadn't put Matt's ashes in an urn but just poured them into the soil so I don't know if what I took was Matt but I had done my best. I put him in a 17th-century Minton china dish, ready to take him home and fulfil his wishes. I carefully replaced the plaque so nobody would know what we had done.

I had to return home then to sort out a few more things, as time was running out. I told the gypsies I'd be back, as I still needed them to arrange my funeral. I had explained what I wanted and left Sharon to prepare it. I knew she would make me proud.

It felt so good to have Matt back with me, although you might think I was mad, and, when I went to bed that night, I put the dish in the bed next to me and took off the lid, and I felt Matt come to me. I felt a connection like I told my John he would feel when he met his dad. Harry Potter getting his wand was just a fairy tale but Matt coming back to me was so real that I felt his presence with me. That night Matt and I became one. Matt was with me, protecting me and loving me. I felt so at peace wrapped up in his presence. Oh, how I had needed him and now I had him and we were soon to be together for all eternity. As I drifted off to sleep, I felt like I was wrapped in his arms again.

The next day I booked a photo shoot for John and me so that he would have some nice photos to remind him of me. We got all dressed up and the photos were beautiful. We had 45 pictures done all together and they were very professional. It was another lovely day I spent with my son and he now had a collection of the most beautiful photos of us together.

I knew that the police were getting worried because I'd heard that people were telling them what I was plotting but I didn't care anymore. I had a policeman come to my home saying he was doing a survey. A likely story! I mean, have you ever heard of that happening? I just welcomed him in and answered his questions. He gave himself away by what he said but I was just polite and played his game. I got the impression he was trying to find out what sort of mental state I was in.

I listened to the radio station Kiss every day, as I had done for the last ten years. But now I noticed they were asking every day for people to come forward if they knew anything about a murder that was about to be committed. It seemed mad that, all of a sudden, they were airing this. It was some sort of police appeal. But again, I just ignored it. It was time to plan how I was going to carry out the killings. I was going to do them all on the same day. One was to happen in Kent, one in the East End and the other two in Essex. I was going to do Ken first and I was going as the Gran in full combat. Then I'd go straight to the East End and do Frank.

I bought a burqa, the Muslim clothing worn by women to cover themselves from head to toe. I would wear it after I had done Ken because I would blend in perfectly in the East End, which was full of Muslims. I would just fit in and nobody would recognise me. All that would show would be my two eyes. Then I would go on to do Bob and Toni.

I bought a wig, contact lenses and a businesswoman's suit to disguise myself. I looked totally different in that get-up. I was going to get close to Bob and Toni's flat without being recognised, then I was going to stab them both through the heart, just as they had done to me. Toni lived on the ground floor and you could look out to the road from her front window. I was going to tie them to chairs, barricade us in and then phone the police. I would open the curtains and wait for the law to come. And when they did, I planned to stab both Bob and Toni. The police would have to shoot me to try and save them and we would all be gone.

I'd got everything I needed and I'd planned it all. But time was running out. The date of 25 August, my court appearance, came and went but I didn't attend. I got a letter from Essex police telling me to hand myself into a police station. It said I had broken the terms of my bail by not appearing. It was time to leave my house and get out of Essex. I couldn't risk getting nicked so I left for Kent and the gypsies. On the way I went to see my son. I knew I was never coming home again. By the end of the month I'd be dead and so would the others. I'd done everything I could to make John's life easier and it was time to go. I grabbed hold of him and, as the tears filled both our eyes, he said, 'Goodbye,' to me. It was the saddest thing I'd ever had to do, waving my boy goodbye and knowing I would never see him again. It broke my heart.

The gypsy queen had done me proud and my funeral had been planned to perfection. My coffin was to be carried from the house in Essex I had shared with Bob to my son's home. Then it would be put into a car and driven to my dad's house in Silvertown, where it would be transferred to a horse-drawn carriage to make the final leg of the journey to the East London cemetery in Plaistow where I would be cremated. All the flowers had been arranged. I'd picked them all. I was to have two swords, two guns and a framed photo of me and Matt placed on my coffin. Oh, it would be beautiful!

I went to say my goodbyes to young Matt and Phoebe. Little Matt didn't want me to go but I had to. I waited for them to fall asleep and I kissed them both goodbye as they slept.

At 6am on 30 August I put all my disguises in Phoebe's car, along with my sword and a combat knife. The blades were razor sharp. I got to Ken's place in

Chilham at about 7am but his garage was shut so I went into a cemetery nearby and read the memorials while I waited. Around 9am I turned my phone on to check for any last messages. I immediately heard interference, followed by the sound of an approaching helicopter. I turned the phone off. It had to be the cops. I knew they were on to me but I didn't care. It looked like they had only sent the helicopter so I stuck to my plan. I could still get Ken, I thought. His garage was on a main road and there wasn't anywhere to park so I planned to use the train station's car park next door. But no sooner had I driven into the car park than loads of police appeared behind me.

'Stop, armed police!' they shouted. I looked round and they were pointing their guns at me. 'Get out of the car. Get out of the car with your hands up.'

I stuck the car into reverse, took off around the police car trying to block me off and out of the station. The chase was on. I was going as fast as I could but I was not familiar with the lanes in Kent and it was not long before I lost control of the car and smashed into a tree. I was unhurt but I couldn't believe what had happened. I was surrounded by police. It had all gone wrong. Matt was waiting for me. But there was no way out of this now, even though I just wanted to be with him.

An officer with a gun approached the front of the car. I grabbed the combat knife, jumped from the car and went for him. 'Shoot me, shoot me!' I screamed like a mad woman as I ran at him brandishing the blade. I wouldn't have hurt him. I don't hurt the innocent. I was just trying to provoke him but then I felt a massive impact from behind. It was like an electric shock. I was losing balance now.

'Shoot me!' I screamed again, still waving the knife but staggering. I just wanted to get with Matt. I was still standing when I felt a second massive hammering sensation in my back. I was lurching like a drunkard, trying to see what had hit me. I was weak now, almost falling but still pleading, 'Shoot me, please shoot...' Then a third hammer blow battered my body. It was like being hit by a lightning strike. That third one did me and I finally slumped and sank to the ground. I was down and I couldn't move. 'Why don't you shoot me?' I asked as they stood over me with their guns. 'Matt's waiting for me and you have ruined everything. What are those stupid things you done me with?'

'Tasers,' one of the officers replied. And he added, 'Jane, it's been ten years since we shot you. Why have you still got the hump with us?'

'I haven't got the hump with yous,' I said. They got me up and cuffed me. 'I'm here to do Ken. He killed Matt. My problem's not with yous.'

I was arrested and taken to Folkstone police station, where I was charged with carrying two offensive weapons, aggravated car theft and affray with the police. I later pleaded guilty to all charges and was sentenced to 18 months at Canterbury crown court. Thanks to my solicitor, Donald Worsley, who was the best in the land in my book as he went that extra mile for me.

I'm glad now that I didn't kill anyone and I'm glad I'm still alive. I believe in my heart and soul that I regained my honour and Matt's honour. It turned out that Ken and his wife had received police protection after he told them what I'd said on my previous little visit. The police had already received tip-offs that I was after Ken. And he ended up needing protection from a woman. I ask you, does it say a lot for him? The police put him into a safe house that morning and he could hardly say he was the man people thought he was.

Then there was Frank. He had me taken off the beach by armed police. I feel he showed me what he was really like.

And, finally, there was Toni and Bob. What could I say about them? To be quite honest, her and Bob deserve one another. She still lives in her flat with her man though so who knows what they are doing now – and who cares? And as for Bob, he turned out to be the biggest letdown of all.

I served just over half of my 18-month sentence at Bronzefield prison in Middlesex and became a free woman again on 14 June 2011. I am now out on licence. The conditions stipulate that I stay away from Ken, Frank, Toni and Bob. If I breach them, I will be back in jail. But I've done enough jail time to last me a lifetime and I don't want to go back.

I'm home now and I'm going to be a grandmother, as

my son is having a baby with his girlfriend. Life goes on. Matt didn't take me that day because it wasn't my time and he can now rest in peace.